EU India relations

This work is published by
Academic Foundation, New Delhi
in association with:

The *Euro* India Centre

EU India relations

a critique

editor: **Shazia Aziz Wülbers**

ACADEMIC FOUNDATION
NEW DELHI

First published in 2008
by

ACADEMIC FOUNDATION
4772-73 / 23 Bharat Ram Road, (23 Ansari Road),
Darya Ganj, New Delhi - 110 002 (India).
Phones : 23245001 / 02 / 03 / 04.
Fax : +91-11-23245005.
E-mail : academic@vsnl.com
www. academicfoundation.com

in association with

The EuroIndia Centre
4, rue Réaumur - 17000 La Rochelle - France
www.euroindia-centre.com

Cataloging in Publication Data--DK
Courtesy: D.K. Agencies (P) Ltd. <docinfo@dkagencies.com>

EU India relations : a critique / editor, Shazia Aziz Wülbers.
p. cm. Contributed articles.
ISBN 13: 9788171886968
ISBN 10: 8171886965

1. India--Foreign economic relations--European Union countries. 2. European Union countries—Foreign economic relations--India. 3. India--Foreign relations—European Union countries. 4. European Union countries --Foreign relations--India. I. Wülbers, Shazia Aziz. II. Title: European Union India relations.
DDC 337.540 4 22

Typeset by Italics India, New Delhi
Printed and bound in India.

Contents

Contributors

Annegret Bendiek
Research Associate, German Institute for International and Security Affairs Berlin, Germany. Email: *Annegret. Bendiek@swp-berlin.org*

Surya Kumar Bose
Director, Bose Information Technology, Hamburg, Germany and member of EuroIndia Centre. Email: *bit@attglobal.net*

Anne Coulon
Deputy Team leader in New Delhi, India on the EU project titled "EU India Trade and Investment Development Programme". She is also attached to the Centre for European Studies at the University of Limerick, Ireland. Email: *anne.coulon@ul.ie*

Rajendra K. Jain
Professor and Director, Europe Area Studies Programme, Centre for European Studies, School of International Studies, Jawaharlal Nehru University, New Delhi. Email: *rkjain13@gmail.com*

Sateesh Kulkarni
Director, Corporate Catalyst India Pvt Ltd., New Delhi, India. Email: *sateesh.kulkarni@gmail.com*

C. Raja Mohan
India's leading Foreign and Security Analyst and Professor at the S. Rajaratnam School of International Studies at Nanyang Technological University, Singapore. Email: *crmohan53@gmail.com*

Sudhanshu Rai

Department of Informatics, Copenhagen Business School, Frederiksberg, Denmark, and member of EuroIndia Centre. Email: *sr.inf@cbs.dk*

Clemens Spiess

Lecturer, South Asia Institute, University of Heidelberg, Germany and former Country Director of the Böll Foundation, New Delhi, India. E-mail: *sclemens@sai.uni-heidelberg.de*

Mario Telo

Director, Institut d'Etudes Européennes, Université Libre de Bruxelles and founder member of European Commission's Garnet network of excellence. Email: *mtelo@ulb.ac.be*

Klaus Julian Voll

Head, India-Europe-Consultancy; former diplomat in the German Embassy in New Delhi and Representative of the Friedrich-Ebert-Foundation in India. Email: *klausvoll@hotmail.com*

Christian Wagner

Senior Research Associate, German Institute for International and Security Affairs, Berlin, Germany. Email: *Christian.Wagner@swp-berlin.org*

Hans Georg Wieck

Chairman, German India Society and Advisory Council of Intelligence Round Table. Email: *hagewie@t-online.de*

Shazia Aziz Wülbers

Editor of EuroIndia Publications and Board member of the EuroIndia Centre. She is also attached to Centre of International Research and Studies at Sciences Po. Email: *shazia.aziz@free.fr*

1

European Union Development Cooperation in India

ANNE COULON

Introduction

"Rising India"—as perceived by some in Europe—has a growth rate that since 1980 ranks amongst the highest in the world, and is now the world's fourth largest economy. Economic reforms in the 1990s have produced a new breed of billionaires. With a population of over one billion, the country supports 20 per cent of the world's people, possesses a growing workforce, and is poised to realise even faster growth in the years to come. India's great advantage in the global marketplace—a large pool of low-wage, educated, English-speaking university graduates—has made it the preferred global hub for software development and business process outsourcing. Yet, despite its recent phenomenal economic progress and important strides for many of the Millennium Development Goals (MDGs), not all share the gains of progress and India still faces the overriding challenge of eradicating endemic poverty. Thirty-five per cent of its population, or the equivalent of more than 300 million people, live on less than $1 a day, and 80 per cent on less than $2. A growing gulf has emerged between Indian states, with the result that poverty is increasingly geographically concentrated: while India's state poverty rates ranged from less than 10 per cent in Goa, Chandigarh and Delhi, for instance, it reaches well above 40 per cent in the two poorest states, Orissa and Bihar.[1] Within the States themselves, socio-economic disparities in education, health, and economic prospects are constantly on the rise,

1. Asian Development Bank (2006). *The Millennium Development Goals: Progress in Asia and the Pacific*. p.9. At: *http://www.adb.org/Documents/Books/MDG-Asia-Pacific/default.asp*

most notably for women and other vulnerable groups. Moreover, India is performing poorly against the health indicators, with the highest total of people living with HIV or AIDS in the world; the virus is spreading quickly, putting the country in danger of a growing epidemic. Prevalence of child and infant mortality rates and of underweight children in the country is amongst the highest in the Asia-Pacific region.[2]

Looking at these disparities, what emerges is a picture of India occupying two worlds simultaneously. [3] In the first, economic reform and social changes are happening and economic growth has a positive impact on citizen's lives; in the other, the population appears to be left behind by the scarcity of public services and the lack of employment opportunities. Bridging the gap between these two Indias is the greatest challenge facing the country today. The subcontinent is, then, by any definition a large state that faces major development challenges, and by virtue of its size and gravity a significant regional actor, one that the EU now sees as an indispensable strategic partner.

This chapter examines the way the EU, which in official documents designates 'strategic partner' India as a 'natural' and 'equal' partner, addresses development challenges in India. The first section looks at the EU's organisational coherence for its development cooperation with India, while subsequent sections respectively examine shifts in development cooperation, before looking at the two-pronged approach to development chosen by the EU to answer to the realities of the two worlds coexisting in India. The concluding sections argue that while the EU is still strongly committed towards fighting against poverty in India via its development cooperation, its strategic interests in making India a partner on the world stage, coupled with India's desire to access EU's markets, prematurely diverts development cooperation efforts and resources towards trade and economic cooperation.

2. Ibid.: 5

3. Quote by Mr. Michael Carter, World Bank's Country Director for India, in "India: World Bank Group Launches New Strategy for India". Press Release No: 2005/60/SAR.

ORGANISATIONAL FRAMEWORK OF EU'S COOPERATION WITH INDIA

Historical Antecedents, Legal Basis and Instruments

In the post-independence period, the scarcity of pledged resources in trade and aid by the then European Economic Community (EEC) in the context of its relations with Asia, reflects the relative disinterest it had for cooperating with the region. The level of aid itself was quite low, mostly subjugated to economic concerns—not given as development assistance but rather in connection to trade, or else as ad-hoc food aid. In any case, before 1993, neither cooperation nor trade arrangements fell under the heading of 'development cooperation', as the EC did not have a legal mandate for this policy area.

The first pillar of EEC 'development policy' was not to be started before the late 1960s, and only in the form of food aid. It was in 1967, in fact, that after the signature by the EEC of the Food Aid Convention, food aid inflows started to be channelled to Asian and Latin American countries. India became the top recipient country of EEC's aid in the 1970–1974 period, with 6.5 per cent of total aid committed. However, this aid still never became too important a factor, with the amounts fading immediately in importance against rising population in India.

Trade, if also meagre in quantitative terms, acted as the bedrock for EU-India relations. In 1981 an Agreement for commercial and economic cooperation was signed,[4] overruling the initial 1973 trade bilateral agreement by covering not only trade but also economic cooperation. Apart from a vague commitment by the Community to "take all possible measures to intensify its support (...) for India's development programs" and the provision establishing the Joint Commission for cooperation, there was little reference to specific policies to be implemented. After 1981, the sectoral allocation of EU aid was developed, and after the first period of almost exclusive food

4. Council of the European Communities (1981). Council Regulation No. 3246/81 on the conclusion of the "Agreement for Commercial and Economic Cooperation between the European Economic Community and India", Collection of the Agreements concluded by the European Communities. Vol. 11, pp.I, 955-972.

aid, extended to rural development in particular, but also education and training. In the meantime, the EU gradually grew to become India's first trading partner and largest foreign inward investor—although, supplanted by ASEAN, it fell back recently to the position of second major trading partner.[5]

It was only with the Maastricht treaty (1992) that the European Community attained a mandate to 'complement' Member States' policies in all aspects of international development. Nevertheless, India did not benefit from the Cotonou Framework for Development[6] and Europe's cooperation approach to Asia and Latin America was encompassed in the Council Regulation (EEC) No. 443/92 of 25th February 1992,[7] which inappropriately grouped Asia and Latin America together.[8]

From Cooperation for Poverty Eradication

In the midst of India's economic reforms and liberalisation, the EU, sensitive to the widespread poverty situation in the country, initiated a new type of external relations, deepening and extending cooperation through a 'third generation EU agreement': the bilateral 1994 Cooperation Agreement on Partnership and Development.[9] Albeit focusing on economic cooperation, the agreement sought to expand relations beyond trade and aid, focusing on poverty reduction as a policy priority, and adding human rights and democratic principles as as components to the relationship. The Agreement marked a turning

---

5. East Asia (i.e. ASEAN plus China, Japan and South Korea) became the first trading partner of India in 2004, accounting for 20 per cent of overall trade, eclipsing the European Union which previously held that position but has fallen back to 19 per cent of overall trade. See Jaffrelot, Christopher (2006). *India and the European Union: The Charade of a Strategic Partnership*, CERI-sciences-Po, Archives. At: *http://www.ceri-sciencespo.com/archive/mars06/art_cj.pdf*

6. The Cotonou framework innovated a partnership with the ACP group, made up of 77 African, Caribbean and Pacific countries.

7. Council of the European Communities (1992). *Council Regulation (EEC)* No. 443/92 of 25th February 1992 on financial and technical assistance to and economic cooperation with developing countries in Asia and Latin America (OJ L 52, 27.2.1992).

8. This Regulation underlined the importance that the Community attaches to the promotion of human rights, support for the process of democratisation, good governance, environmental protection, trade liberalisation and strengthening the cultural dimension, by means of an increasing dialogue on political, economic and social issues conducted in mutual interest.

9. Council of the European Communities Cooperation Agreement (1994). *Cooperation Agreement between the European Community and the Republic of India on Partnership and Development* (OJ L 223/24, 27.8.94)

point in the relations between the EU and India with provisions such as the extent of institutionalised economics and political cooperation assuming prominence (with the joint political statement simultaneously agreed). It laid down a development strategy focused on supporting poverty reduction projects, promoting a more efficient and sustainable use of resources, with sector programmes aimed at improving basic social services, including health and education.

The legal framework for EU development policy was reaffirmed by Article 177 of the 1997 Amsterdam Treaty (ex Article 130u of the Maastricht Treaty), defining the priorities as: "sustainable economic and social development in favour of developing countries, with a particular emphasis on the most disadvantaged countries; progressive and harmonious integration of developing countries in the world economy; and fighting poverty in developing countries." Five years after the Maastricht Treaty, in formal terms, the poverty reduction objective was still one among three equally strong objectives of EC development cooperation.

The EU development policy was reframed around the objective of eradicating poverty with the November 2000 Council of the European Union and the European Commission (EC)'s joint statement on the European Community's Development Policy.[10] The latest determined a number of areas selected on the basis of their contribution towards reducing poverty and for which Community action provides added value. The Statement was then revised in the form of the European Consensus on Development signed on 20th December 2005 which reaffirmed the poverty eradication objective in the context of development, in line with the international agenda of the MDGs.

In terms of instruments, programming of EC aid is centred on the Country Strategy Paper (CSP), the geographical and main programming document—although it still leaves aside thematic budget lines related to NGO project financing.[11] The first EU-India CSP,

---

10. *The European Community's Development Policy*. Statement by the Council and the Commission (2000). At *http://europa.eu.int/comm/development/body/legislation/docs/council_statement.pdf*

11. CSPs set out a 'strategic framework' for the EC's central priorities in a given country and region covering both development assistance and other essential activities ('the policy mix'). The CSP/RSPs are developed at the delegation level in collaboration with national governments, members states, other bilateral and multilateral donors, and wherever

(contd...)

covering the period 2002-2006, in line with European legislation, pursued the 1994 Cooperation Agreement's philosophy to have as its overall guiding principle the elimination of poverty. As part of the strategy, the EC committed itself to assist India in: "improving health services in favour of hitherto deprived population groups; making elementary education universal; restoring and safeguarding a healthy environment; and helping communities at risk to be better prepared for disasters."[12]

To Cooperation as a 'Policy Mix' Embodied in a Wider Strategy for Partnership

In 2004, the overall EU cooperation strategy with India experienced a shift with Commission Communication on an EU-India Strategic Partnership of June of the same year. The Communication, launching the strategic Partnership between the EU and India, linked the issues of poverty, sustainable economic growth and enhanced trade, combining these into sector programmes of economic cooperation and development cooperation. The subsequent Joint Action Plan (JAP), adopted as a roadmap for the operationalisation of the Partnership at the last EU-India Summit (7th September 2005), outlined concrete actions to implement the Partnership and featured provisions on cooperation.

These elements suggest that economic cooperation and development cooperation, beyond the results they may produce, are an element in a wider strategy that aims at supporting the achievement of EU strategic objectives. They will inevitably imbue the writing and content of the next CSP for 2007-2013 (currently being drafted by the Commission services).

(contd...)

possible, with representatives of civil society. CSPs should be based on national development strategies drawn up by recipient governments. The adoption by the European Commission of the CSPs and National Indicative Plans (NIPs) marked an attempt to address some of the problems that had become apparent in the EU's previous development approach, by focusing specifically on particular countries in question. The incentive was to improve the coherence of the policy toward third countries—particularly, to ensure a match between EU political priorities and spending on development assistance. A fragmented and project-based aid culture was to be replaced by comprehensive country analysis and strategic approaches to aid programming. In policy papers and political rhetoric at least, local ownership and participation became acknowledged as the key for aid effectiveness.

12. *EC Country Strategy Paper India*. 10 September 2002. At: *http://ec.europa.eu/comm/external_relations/india/csp/02_06en.pdf*

Key Actors in EU-India Cooperation

The Ministers for development cooperation of the Member States take decisions in the Council of Ministers, while the European Parliament (EP)'s resolutions and reports have an impact on the conduct of EU-India cooperation. But it is the EC that plays a leading role in development cooperation. As the executive body of the European Community, the EC manages its development assistance. It negotiates trade and cooperation agreements with outside countries and groups of countries, on behalf of the Union. Because of its right of initiative to put policy proposals to Member States, the EC is also charged with making proposals in the development cooperation area.

At the EC, the remit of the cooperation with India does not fall under DG Development. Relations with Asia and Latin America are managed by the Directorate General for External Relations (DG Relex)—with foreign policy objectives potentially dominating as a consequence. The 'geographical' DG Relex is responsible for the pluri-annual programming of external assistance to India. Brussels is giving the impulse regarding actions to be taken regarding India to its Delegation through Unit 3: "India, Bhutan, Nepal", of the Directorate H (Asia, except Japan and Korea), under the supervision of the Director General. Additionally, the EC Directorate General for Humanitarian Aid (ECHO) provides financial assistance in response to conflicts or natural disasters in third countries, solely on the basis of their humanitarian needs assessments and is active in relation to India, and has an office in Delhi.[13]

In India, besides its traditional role of political representation, the EC Delegation, in accordance with the principle that anything that can better be managed and decided on the spot in the country concerned should be done there and not in Brussels,[14] has seen its role substantially enhanced. Due to 'deconcentration', the management of external aid was devolved from the headquarters to its structure in

---

13. In October 2005, a devastating earthquake hit Pakistan and India, killing 75,000 people. Almost €14 million were allocated in the first weeks after the disaster and additional funds were rapidly mobilised, in particular from the European Commission's emergency reserve. DG ECHO was able to allocate €48.6 million before the end of the year. At: *http://ec.europa.eu/comm/external_relations/reform/document/communication_en.pdf*

14. Commission of the European Communities (2000). "Communication to the Commission on the Reform of the Management of External Assistance". 16 May. rev. 8.

2002. The Delegation manages the whole range of economic and development cooperation programmes supported by the EU in the country (education, health, environment, trade and investment facilitation, Civil Society and NGO-related projects). It also develops and implements the National Indicative Programmes (NIPs) and CSPs. Furthermore, the Delegation maintains contacts with authorities in India/Nepal/Bhutan and with project partners, which may be the Central government, or one of the state governments or an NGO, on the one hand, and is co-coordinating all activities with the EC headquarters in Brussels, on the other.

For coordination purposes, monthly or bi-monthly coordination meetings involving development officers from both the Delegation and EU Embassies are organised by the EU Presidency. In addition, there are frequent coordination meetings between EC officers and representatives from DFID[15] and GTZ[16], with the UK and Germany being the main donors among the EU Member States.

EuropeAid Cooperation Office—AIDCO—in Brussels supervises deconcentrated activities and provides support (technical, financial, contractual) to the Delegation. Completing the institutional framework; the EC-India Joint Commission, created by the 1994 Cooperation Agreement, oversees cooperation activities. The Joint Commission is in practice mainly a meeting place for Indian and EC representatives and technical advisers, to which report three separate sub-commissions: on trade, economic cooperation and development cooperation.

THE EU'S DEVELOPMENT APPROACH TO INDIA: CHARACTERISTICS AND QUALITATIVE SHIFTS

EC Financial and Sectoral Commitments to Development in India

There has always been a strong political/foreign policy element in EC aid, reflecting EC strategic priorities. The late 1990s showed an increased aid to Central and Eastern Europe, the Balkans and the

15. The Department for International Development (DFID) is the British Government Department responsible for international development.

16. German government agency for technical cooperation. At: *http://ec.europa.eu/europeaid/reports/europeaid_annual_report_2006_full_version_en.pdf*

Mediterranean countries. In 1998-99, European Community aid to Asia fell to a low of only seven per cent of total EC funds. However, from 2001 to 2005, the volume of committed aid towards Asia doubled, shadowing aid to the Balkans, but still lagging behind the Mediterranean countries.[17]

If European Community assistance funding is channelled partly through the regular budget of the Commission and partly via the European Development Fund (EDF), assistance to countries in Asia, Latin America, the Mediterranean and Central and Eastern Europe, is financed from budgetary aid, i.e. the regular budget of the Commission. It is important to note that, if the EU and its Member States bilateral actions collectively make the biggest bilateral contribution to India's development programmes, the EC is a relatively small donor in India. Moreover, the EC unblocks co-financing with non-governmental organisations through horizontal/thematic budget lines, besides geographic instruments, (Budget Line 21 02 03 ex-B7-6000).

The India programme of cooperation is the largest country programme within the ALA region. EC assistance to India is entirely in the form of grants (that include technical assistance in the form of monitoring and evaluation, consultants, training, etc.). Resources committed during 1993-2000 amounted to €837 million, but fell down for the period 2000 to 2006 with a budget of €430 million.[18] Nonetheless, in 2004, India ranked as the 11th EC recipient aid country, while it was only at the 15th position of non-EC aid in the same year.[19] The particular attention given to India not only reflects the EU's philanthropy but also its strategic priorities.

Altogether, 12 projects in rural development have been run by the EC, for a total amounting to €240 million, with a focus on poverty

---

17. A sharp rise was recorded with commitments to Asia almost doubling over 2004: €6.2 billion in development aid was disbursed, up from €5.7 billion the year before. Commission of the European Communities (2006). *Annual Report 2006 on the European Community's Development Policy and the Implementation of External Assistance in 2005* At: *http://ec.europa.eu/europeaid/reports/europeaid_annual_report_2006_full_version_en.pdf*

18. Consortium Eva-EU c/o NCG (May 2002). "Evaluation of Council Regulation N.443/92 on Co-operation between the EC and ALA countries, Final Report." At: *http://ec.europa.eu/comm/europeaid/evaluation/reports/ala/951614.pdf*

19. Development Strategies Consultancy (2006). "EU Donor Atlas", Volume I, Mapping Official Development Assistance, February. At: *http://ec.europa.eu/comm/development/body/publications/docs/eu_donor_atlas_2006.pdf*

alleviation. This approach has been phased out and replaced with sector wide budget support approach to social development. €240 million has been pledged for the health sector, and €350 million in elementary education. Finally, €160 million has been pledged to the multi sector policy support Programme aiming at poverty alleviation via the State Partnership Programme to the States of Chhattisgarh and Rajasthan.

Furthermore, EC cooperation (through grants awarded following calls for proposals on different thematic issues) has been reaching civil society and the NGO community, also building bridges between European and Indian NGOs. Currently 118 projects are ongoing, totalling €65 million. The majority of these projects directly address poverty reduction, while others are focusing on reproductive health and HIV/AIDS, as well as tropical forests which are strongly interrelated with the livelihoods of tribal people in several regions and States of India.

From Project-Based to Sector-Wide Budget Support Approach (SWAP)

In the initial stages, the EC's development assistance was in the form of project financing. However, in the mid-1990s, EC-India cooperation was redirected towards identified priority sectors for action: primary education and primary healthcare, through a sector-wide approach (SWAP) in both education (since 1993) and health (since 1996). This sectoral approach was complemented by support for focused projects in rural and natural resource development.

The EC rural programme in India includes projects in (i) land reclamation, (ii) forestry, (iii) integrated watershed development, (iv) irrigation, and (v) agricultural production and marketing. Most of the projects concerning rural development and natural resources are now completed or are on their way towards completion. Even though their relative dispersion has limited sectoral policy impact, they have produced some visible impacts and had poverty reduction as their central focal point. For instance, the rural development "Doon Valley" project stopped land degradation, improved farming methods and management of natural resources, reaching an area covering some 300 villages with a population of about 400,000 people. This project was one of the EU-funded projects that were adopted as models for larger schemes funded by the World Bank.

The EC chose to adopt a sector-wide approach for its certain advantages over a project-based approach. Sectoral programmes are expected to ensure better policy dialogue with the Government of India (GoI) and coordination with other donors, as well as easier disbursements: technically the latter are done in the form of budgetary support, though they are not actually classified as such. Other advantages include a wider impact, more local ownership and better chances of sustainability. Such an approach also requires that donors have sufficient confidence in the capacity of the beneficiary country's administration to manage sector-wide programmes and to account for their implementation, results and costs.[20] However, when the EC introduced its SWAP in heath and education, there was no precedent in India in these areas.

To overcome the lack of common reporting, accounting and auditing systems, in the nationwide education system, EC funds were allocated to a single Indian state (Rajasthan) and specific structures in that state were also created. The programme, called District Primary Education Programme (DPEP) was allocated a grant of €150 million and finished in 2002. The DPEP focused on the poorest and most deprived children, with emphasis on education for girls. Building on the success of the DPEP, EU-India collaboration on education then continued through EC support to the Government's Sarva Shiksha Abhiyan (SSA), launched in 2001-2002. GoI's target was to universalise access to, and completion of elementary education (Grades 1-8) of satisfactory quality by 2010, in order to comply with the Millennium Development Goals of Education for All (EFA). SSA was designed to provide a comprehensive policy and budgetary framework for achieving the aforementioned objectives. Also, one of the over-arching goals of the SSA is to bridge all gender and social gaps by 2010. To achieve this, SSA offers area-specific and tribe-

20. Court of Auditors (2003). "Special Report No 10/2003 concerning the effectiveness of the Commission's management of development assistance to India in targeting the poor and ensuring sustainable benefits, together with the Commission's replies" (OJ, C211/21, 5.9.2003).

specific interventions to meet the learning needs of tribal children.[21] The total cost of the project is estimated as being approximately €18 billion (2001-2010). Following discussions for external funding, in early 2003, the United Kingdom/DFID (€270 million), World Bank/ IDA (€390 million), and the European Commission (€200 million) agreed with the GoI (€3.1 billion) to pool funds and support the SSA in a sector-wide approach (SWAP) between 2004 and 2007.

For the health sector programme, one of the main challenges was to link health policy (which are the responsibilities of the States) to family welfare (joint responsibility of the state and the central government), and overcome the lack of coordination in the health sector. District health agencies were set up in 20 districts as a pilot project, and health policy became more prominent in the 10th and 11th five-year plans—testifying to the impact of the policy reform process. This also meant that the GoI would be able to provide the EC with up-to-date and audited financial statements on the overall health programme.

The EC committed €240 million into India's Health and Family Welfare Sector Investment Programme (SIP) over the period 1997-2006. An integral part of the Government's National Family Welfare Programme, the SIP's aim is to reform the Indian health care system by focusing on primary health care services and, in particular, to enhance the quality and access of health care services for disadvantaged groups. The programme has been developed into a sector wide programme encompassing all family welfare activities and bringing together all supporting donors. The subsequent EC Programme on Reproductive and Child Health was further aimed at helping States to make a paradigm shift away from the target-oriented family planning approach to a more holistic health care system, focusing in particular on women and children. This EC-supported programme is results orientated based on the broad principles of a participative, emergent and iterative process of identifying primary areas of health reform. EC funds have provided flexibility since the

21. Address by Mr. Francisco Da Câmara Gomes, Ambassador and Head of Delegation of the European Commission On the Occasion of the Thematic Seminar "Reaching out to the Tribal Communities in India: The European Commission's Experience". India Habitat Centre, New Delhi. 28 June 2006

grant is not tied to any particular programme component as long as the component has been designed through the participatory process with due regard to sustainability.

From SWAPs to State Partnerships (SPP)

After shifting its bilateral development cooperation focus from a project based to a sector based approach, the EC developed a partnership approach with 'reform-minded States'.[22] The approach made sense in a context of the political decentralisation in India, which started in the 1990s, whereby States became in charge of controlling 90 per cent of development resources.[23] Decentralisation brought a general shift in dynamics within India from the centre towards individual State Governments. What is more, given the complexity of the political and administrative situation in India, local support became imperative for the success of programmes on the ground. Shifting towards a SWAP approach was also for the EC a means to make a significant impact on poverty by concentrating its scarce resources on one or two States and to have by the same occasion a possibility to mainstream its comprehensive package of values and principles in development. As the CSP 2002-2006 noted:

> "The key question for all external donors, the EC included, remains how to achieve a significant impact on poverty given India's vastness and administrative and political complexity ... it is now the States that control 90 per cent of development resources that determine how policies are implemented on the ground. Experience from these project units and programmes should feed back into policy decision making and serve as replicable models for larger scale interventions by the Government of India."

In keeping with this, the EC planned to invest its resources in a "Partnership for Progress" with "reform-minded" Indian States "committed to reducing poverty by pursuing a social and economic

22. *EC Country Strategy Paper India, op. cit..*: 25
23. The approach is similar to DFID's one, the latest having state partnership with four of India's states: Orissa, Andhra Pradesh, Madhya Pradesh, and West Bengal, going back as far as more than 20 years in the case of Orissa.

reform agenda."[24] The State Partnerships (SPP) are meant to be a catalyser of state-level reforms, offering a state level sector-wide development approach, with the core components of basic health and elementary education, improved governance as an overarching agenda, and environment as a crosscutting component. They aim to supplement the efforts of the GoI and state governments to accelerate progress towards the MDGs.

In the general context of international aid, the States most favoured by aid have traditionally not necessarily been the poorest; for a long time, states such as Bihar, Orissa and Uttar Pradesh were condemned by the stereotype equating poor with poor performing. Although it was agreed by the EC and the GoI that support was to be brought to the neediest states, the EC also developed some specific selection criteria to work through a comprehensive work aid package with a consenting state. It determined that the chosen state had to belong to this group of reforming States who "pioneered policies that are conducive to economic growth, including fiscal and civil service reform, domestic and foreign investment facilitation and overall improved governance."[25] Moreover, the state had to answer to four criteria: welcome EC cooperation, be situated in the lower half of the GDP ranking of Indian states and showing a deficit in the balance of social indicators, embrace a strategy to tackle gender and discrimination issues show commitment to reducing poverty at the centre of a strategy to improve public finances and service delivery. The assessment study concluded that both Rajasthan and Chhattisgarh were the most suitable states for engaging in a 'State Partnership'.

The new 'Partnership for Progress' approach was approved by the GoI in May 2002. A Memorandum of Understanding was signed with the EC on 25/2/2004, and the SPP was made part of the 2nd India NIP (2004-06).

In Chhattisgarh, where 32 per cent of the total population is tribes, the SPP is expected to provide for an integrated approach to the development. The EC's sector budget support and technical assistance

24. *EC Country Strategy Paper India, op. cit.:* 3

25. Ibid.: 25

will expedite the Government of Chhattisgarh's efforts to develop and implement comprehensive reforms in the education sector and deepen reform initiatives in the health and family welfare sector. It also intends to create an enabling pro-poor environment policy framework and enhanced capacities, specifically addressing non-timber forest-based tribal livelihoods.

In Rajasthan, also called the 'desert state', water scarcity has emerged as the single most critical determinant to development across different sectors, including health and education. The EC grant is intended to support the Government of Rajasthan in refining and implementing its new Water Resources Policy, which aims at an integrated management approach and a larger role for local communities in water resources management. The objective is to ensure the provision of safe, adequate and sustainable drinking water for the people of Rajasthan. A novel feature of the SPP is its support to the Government's multi-stakeholder consultation and awareness campaign to ensure public participation in the design and implementation of the water policy.

EU POLICY DESIGN: THE RATIONALE OF A TWO-PRONGED APPROACH TO DEVELOPMENT

Economic Cooperation: Superseding Development Cooperation?

The Commission is steadily moving towards a strategic but transitional approach, away from traditional development assistance. The emphasis is placed on economic and trade related assistance and civil society exchange in a bid to be coherent with both the needs of the 'new' India and the EU-India bilateral strategic partnership.

In the context of the EU's external relations with Asia, there is a clear distinction between economic cooperation and development cooperation. In fact, economic cooperation exists for a long time, for in the 1980s and 1990s, direct contacts between European agents and their counterparts in more developed partner States were facilitated by the European Community, in order to establish direct partnerships at the level of economic operators.[26] This approach in international economic relations; i.e. the enhancement of partnerships between autonomous, social, public and private groups, was initiated in 1991 with the Council conclusions setting guidelines for cooperation with Asian and Latin American developing countries for the 1990s.[27] The EC's official sources then presented economic cooperation as a component of its external relations, together with other elements such as development cooperation, security or cultural policies. This new spirit corresponded to a will to add new elements to the existing situation of one-way financial transfers from Europe;[28] and the Declaration of 8 June 2000 on a new strategic partnership between the EU and India integrated this, highlighting the need for extended economic cooperation. [29]

The 1994 Cooperation Agreement had already made clear the objective of an economic cooperation 'of the widest possible scope in order to contribute to the expansion of their (EU and India's) respective economies and their developmental needs'.[30] In this perspective, economic cooperation aimed at building sustainable relations with the country; in contrast to development cooperation seen as a more asymmetric and temporary relation with the aim of modifying the socio-economic situation.

That being said, the EC approach to support of the private sector in the context of development aid is not directed in the first instance towards the development of business-to-business relations but towards the reduction of poverty.[31] Economic cooperation with India,

---

26. The autonomy of social groups: public authorities, and profit and non-profit private actors and their level of involvement in direct partnerships facilitated by the EC were decisive in supporting partnership links.

27. These guidelines are contained in COM (1995) 495 on perspectives of the partnership with Latin America for the period of 1996-2000 and COM (2001) 469 on the strategic framework for enhanced partnership between Europe and Asia.

28. ADE (2002). "Clarifying the Definitions of EC Economic Co-operation with Third Countries". At: *http://web.particip.de/pac-rep/voletb/docs/axe1/951636.pdf*

29. *europa.eu.int/comm./external_relations/india/eco/index.htm*

30. It was in this spirit that the EC-India Summit of 8 June 2000 witnessed a Declaration on new strategic partnership between these two entities.

31. The same is true for the reduction of trade barriers, which are also designed as nonreciprocal since, in the case of LDCs; immediate mutual interest is superseded by the priority given to poverty reduction.

in the first CSP (2002-2006), was envisaged as a 'special responsibility' for the EU to help India undertake the 'second generation' of economic reforms, help it unlock its full economic potential, through sharing good practice in economic governance and efforts to integrate its economy regionally and with the global economy. In the CSP 2002-2006, both development and economic cooperation were seen as essential components of an effective strategy aimed at the elimination of poverty, through equitable economic growth on the basis of sustainable development.

Nonetheless, the transition from 'economic cooperation' as a mere instrument of helping to lift India out of poverty, to 'economic cooperation' as an area of mutual interest in sectors where India is bound to become a key partner for the EU, has gradually been happening- at least on paper. The 2005 JAP focuses on the importance of strengthening dialogue on matters of mutual interest in areas of economic cooperation to improve the business environment, leading to strengthened economic relations. More economic cooperation presents two main advantages: it leads in the long run to more bilateral trade and investment, which is beneficial to the EU and India alike. There is also a more strategic advantage attached to it: it can help overcome different internal concerns that often direct their respective external policies in different directions, making a partnership more difficult to manage. This type of cooperation serves the EU strategic objective of making India an ally on world stage forums.

The draft CSP 2007-2013 reflects this position. It contains the 'policy mix' that the EC sees necessary to maximise its strategic objectives. In this mix, cooperation is not seen as an end in itself, but rather as an element in a strategy that aims at attaining the bilateral objectives agreed in the 2004 Commission Communication and embodied in the JAP. The objectives relate more to strategic issues, to the two entities becoming closer allies in international trade and political forums and moves away from the previous aid rhetoric that had no objective beyond the eradication of poverty. The CSP is referred to by EC officials as 'transitional' because of the clear shift from development assistance towards cultural and economic cooperation between India and the EC. In the new country strategy, the EU's cooperation approach gives growing importance to economic reforms and policy dialogue with the EU in sectors such as energy, transport and the environment as policy areas of mutual interest. This approach is coherent with the JAP, which promotes sectoral dialogue and joint projects in the aforementioned areas. Sectoral dialogue and joint projects with good governance as the cross cutting theme are in the draft CSP 2007-2013 projected to mobilise around 10 per cent of the funding foreseen with NIP I, and double by increasing to around 20 per cent in NIP II. One can fear that sectors like infrastructure, transport and macroeconomic support take precedence over health, education or food security, as overviews of CSPs tend to show. This makes evidence of both the need for complementarity between geographical instruments and thematic budget lines, and the important role of NGOs in strengthening civil society and poverty-focused objectives.

Nonetheless, it is very inaccurate to say that 'traditional' development cooperation has vanished, and that the poverty component has disappeared from the EU's cooperation approach. The EU is seeing its approach as a two-pronged one, designed to deal with an India that is 'occupying two worlds at the same time'. In the forthcoming CSP, development cooperation still mobilises the main bulk of EU cooperation funding, with social sector funding (health and education) foreseen at 62 per cent of the CSP/NIP 2007-2013 and the Implementation of the Action Plan (Economic Sectoral Dialogues and Cooperation Civil Society and Cultural Exchanges and Academic Exchanges) at 38 per cent of CSP/NIP.[32]

A significant increase of development cooperation for the social sectors, i.e. the universalisation of elementary education (Sarva Shiksa Abhiyan) and the National Rural Health Mission of the Government of India shall even be expected in the context of the 2007-2013 CSP. Poverty alleviation is central to these sectors, and even if concentrated on two States, testifies of the prominence of development cooperation.

Is the new cooperation strategy understood and approved by both India and the EU, and more importantly, accurate to India's developmental needs?

32. DG Relex, Presentation "7th European Diplomatic Programme Module II", 25/10/2006.

India's Reactions

From the EC point of view, the EU and India are increasingly equal partners; both enabled to jointly face global challenges and play similar roles. The EU's stance towards development cooperation rests on the observations that if India is to continue on its current path of rapid economic development, the need for future development assistance will clearly diminish. With this approach, it is understood that future CSPs should focus more and more on areas of mutual interest and, eventually, reach a point when development assistance is not required any more. The approach is in some extent supported by the GoI. While appreciating EU development efforts in the country, recent interaction (Action Plan seminar) between the EC and GoI officials showed Indian officials keen interest in accessing EC know-how and to learn from lessons learned and best practices. India feels that developing countries have to be provided access to markets and a 'level playing field', and also, an access to technology. In this context, it is welcoming economic cooperation with the EU as a means of accelerating its own development objectives and extending its economic prospects with the wider world. It is also, and most importantly, a way for the GoI to improve its access to the EU market. Moreover, while the EC along with other donors has been concerned about the limited impact of its aid programmes in India, the GoI has consistently advocated that the way to address this problem was through 'trade, not aid', encouraging the move from aid to economic cooperation. In this context, economic cooperation fits in well with a rhetoric designating trade as the key to successful development.

Notwithstanding this approach, the Indian discourse on external development assistance has changed in the last few years, showing successive and somewhat contradictory shifts. In September 2003, under the then nationalistic Bharatiya Janata Party-led Government, India positioned itself to the world as an 'aid giver', with the GoI announcing new guidelines for development cooperation with bilateral partners. As per the new guidelines, India was to receive direct bilateral assistance only from Japan, the United Kingdom, Germany, the United States of America, the EC and the Russian Federation. All other bilateral assistance was to be routed either through multilateral organisations, or for projects of economic and social importance directly to universities, NGOs or autonomous bodies registered under the Foreign Contribution (Regulation) Act.

Then, with the new United Progressive Alliance (UPA)'s government currently in power, a significant shift in India's approach occurred, with the current government quickly back-pedalling on the previous government's decision to limit cooperation to only six bilateral donors (including the EC). Firstly, the select group of bilateral donors was expanded to include all G-8 Countries. Secondly, it was decided that small bilateral donors who are not part of the G-8 would be accepted if their contributions exceed $25 million per year. Then, the Finance Ministry promised to submit new, more transparent guidelines for cooperation with NGOs.

Last but not the least, on 29th July 2005, the GoI requested a €2 billion contribution from the EU to its health and education programmes, which constitutes the most remarkable shift in India's stance towards development assistance and indeed the first time the GoI makes an appeal at the highest level for a substantial increase of EC development cooperation in these (or other) sectors. This demarche is unique in that it makes an official appeal for assistance at the highest level (directly by the Prime Minister Manmohan Singh). The EC, not in the position to accede to India's demand, attempted to reassure India at the 5th bilateral Summit on the fact that in its new CSP covering 2007-2013 it would continue its commitment to the social sectors- and to the health sector in particular. It is important to note that in the demarche Indian officials did not question the EU's economic cooperation efforts, aware of the potential of such cooperation for India, and of its long term outcomes. Yet, the demand itself, expressed under the rubric of a dialogue on strategic partnership, says a great deal about the difficulties for India to meet the MDGs and about its continued need for development assistance. India is performing very poorly against the MDGs and seeks to give a positive signal at the forthcoming Millennium Review Summit.

Relevance of the Model of EU Cooperation?

Is the EU cooperation approach appropriate in the Indian context? The 2005 European Consensus on Development, as seen above, states that the primary and overarching objective of EU development cooperation is the eradication of poverty in the context of sustainable development, including the pursuit of the MDGs. Although the EU-India development cooperation is inclined to follow these objectives in the SPP framework, there is a worrying decline in the new instruments in favour of economic cooperation, on the basis of a partnership of 'equals'. The shift seems to be premature in a country that is home to a quarter of the world's truly destitute. Although the appreciation of these programmes by the GoI is substantial, and generates considerable visibility for the EC, one can wonder how relevant they are to the poverty situation of the country.

The European apparel itself manifests its concerns with the EP extorting the EC to maintain the MDGs and combating poverty as a 'central element of the EU-India Strategic Partnership' in its report in September 2006 on economic and trade relations with India.[33] But are CSPs strong enough as instruments to address poverty issues? In a context where much is decided between GoI officials and EC officials, development programming is inevitably influenced by internal political interests and financial concerns rather than being driven by the rights and needs of the poorest.

The first CSP 2002-2006 had previously raised some concerns and criticisms. Much of the work on the drafting of the document was done in Brussels, over a six month period, drawing on the guidelines of the Inter-Service Quality Support Group (IQSG). According to an EU official, 'it was more an internal Commission exercise rather than a collaborative bilateral one'.[34] Based upon an analysis and assessment of the Indian national development strategy done in Brussels, it was strongly informed by the Commission's internal considerations of policy guidance and recommendations, and written under the pressure of time.[35] The participation of civil society groups was largely disregarded.

Beyond this, there were also concerns about how the issue of poverty had been addressed by the EC in its strategy paper. The

33. European Parliament (2006). *Report on the EU's Economic and Trade Relations with India*, (2006/2034 (INI)). Committee on International Trade Rapporteur: Sajjad Karim, FINAL, A6-0256/2006.

34. Interview held on the phone on the 20th of April 2005 with a EU Official (No.1).

35. Interview held on the phone with an other EU official (No.2), 20th April 2005

Commission's chief critic, the European Court of Auditors, issued a report in late 2003,[36] charging the EC with failing to properly address key poverty-cause issues. Among others, it accused the European Commission of having overlooked its own policy on fighting rural poverty as laid down in the 2002 EC's Communication,[37] leaving aside the key sectors of agriculture and natural resources management.[38] It is tempting to attribute this lacuna to negligence on the part of the EC especially when looking at the next developments in cooperation; i.e. what can be seen as the somewhat reductionist solution to synthesise development cooperation objectives in two sectors and two States. In reality, overlooking structural causes of poverty in India might have been due to the EU having a liberal infused approach to development and progress, in a context where the State still has an overwhelming role to play. The EU's advice to combat large fiscal deficits of the central and state governments drew upon a liberal solution, by proposing that Indian authorities control fiscal deficits (in practice, a reduction in government expenditure), liberalising trade, fiscal restructuring, increasing public sector efficiency, and reducing the role of the State in agriculture, industry, transport and energy. Nonetheless, the draft CSP 2007-2013 adopts a progressive discourse more relevant to the needs of the subcontinent's people. In the country economic analysis identified the delivery of pro-poor policies, including employment guarantees and the analysis focus on the promotion of the rural economy as well as good governance as the biggest challenge for the UPA Government, and as a part of a large unfinished agenda it needs to tackle.

In the meantime, the EU is seeking to induce changes in two 'laboratory' States. A sum of €160 million was planned to be allocated to the two SPP. The amount is to be halved between the two States at the starting point, but in case a State lags behind in the 'race', it will lose a portion of its share to the other. Here lies a manifest contradiction whereby a poorer performing state—which may be

36. Court of Auditors (2003). *op. cit.*

37. Commission Communication (2002). *Fighting Rural Poverty: European Community Policy and Approach to Rural Development and Sustainable Natural Resource Management in Developing Countries*. COM (2002) 429, Bull. 7/8-2002

38. Court of Auditors (2003). *op. cit.*

performing more slowly due to higher capacity investment requirements—is as a result facing reduced financial support when more is required.

The GoI, at odds with the EC's SPP approach itself, and which favours a top-down approach to development, made an appeal to the EU for it to re-orientate its aid through multi-state organisations rather than being geographically determined.[39] In any case, the relevance of SPP can be questioned as the SPP can be seen as shifting away development aid from the poorest sections of the Indian population in the poorest states.

Conclusion

For the period 2007-2013, the forthcoming developments of EU development cooperation in India are centered on two themes: the continued and enhanced support of the social sectors of health, SWAPs and SPPs on the one side, and cooperation through the implementation of the EU-India Partnership Joint Action Plan on the other. This reflects the two-pronged approach the EU chose to maximise its impact on India's poverty and India's integration in the world economy. The EC is now seeking to provide support that could generate maximum added value. Its aim is to become instrumental in contributing to the reform process and better policy-making so as to have a lasting impact in India. The EU's relationship with India is better understood in the context of a broader strategic agenda. For this purpose it has chosen to focus on a limited number of key sectors, and to clean the portfolio of non-strategic activities. Whether the whole approach is likely to have a tangible impact on the eradication of poverty in India by 2013, is another question. India needs further economic reforms and institutional change to adapt to an interdependent international economy. The EU's economic cooperation can be instrumental in addressing the country's challenge of poor roads and insufficient water and electricity supplies, all of which could thwart its development. But then again, the EC sees itself and is in quantitative terms a relatively small donor for a country such as India, and it is in its interest to generate as much impact as possible.

39. GoI (2004). EC Communication titled *An EU-India Strategic Partnership: India's Response*. At: *http://meaindia.nic.in/onmouse/EU-Indian.pdf*

In India, there is considerably greater scope for donor involvement, in partnership with the GoI, in States which perform poorly on poverty reduction or human development, in addition to those where effectiveness has improved because of political change. Also, with a mostly rural population, the agricultural sector needs to be further supported. While a number of conditions determine how much the poor share in the country's growth, the extent to which growth stems from the rural areas, particularly agriculture, is key. However, growth in the agricultural sector is lagging behind. The EU might not be able to address these problems on its own, but synergies with other donors, not least EU Member States, could make more significant inroads on poverty.

References

Official Documents

Commission of the European Communities (2000). Communication to the Commission on the *Reform of the Management of External Assistance*. 16 May. rev. 8. At *http://ec.europa.eu/comm/external_relations/reform/document/communication_en.pdf*

———. (2002). Communication from the Commission- *Fighting rural poverty - European Community policy and approach to rural development and sustainable natural resource management in developing countries.* COM (2002) 429, Bull. 7/8-2002.

———. (2006). *Annual Report 2006 on the European Community's Development Policy and the Implementation of External Assistance in 2005.* At *http://ec.europa.eu/europeaid/reports europeaid_annual_ report_2006_full _version_en.pdf*

Council of the European Communities (1981). Council Regulation No 3246/81 on the *Conclusion of the Agreement for Commercial and Economic Cooperation between the European Economic Community and India.* Collection of the Agreements concluded by the European Communities. Vol. 11.

———. (1992). Council Regulation (EEC) No. 443/92 of 25th February 1992 on *Financial and Technical Assistance to and Economic Cooperation with the Developing Countries in Asia a=And Latin America* (OJ L 52, 27.2.1992).

Council of the European Communities Cooperation Agreement (1994). *Cooperation Agreement between the European Community and the Republic of India on Partnership and Development* (OJ L 223/24, 27.8.94).

European Parliament (2006). *Report on the EU's Economic and Trade Relations with India* (2006/2034(INI)) Committee on International Trade Rapporteur: Sajjad Karim. FINAL, A6-0256/2006.

Court of Auditors (2003). *Special Report No 10/2003 concerning the effectiveness of the Commission's management of development assistance to India in targeting the poor and ensuring sustainable benefits, together with the Commission's replies* (OJ, C211/21, 5.9.2003).

The European Community's Development Policy: Statement by the Council and the Commission (2000). At *http://europa.eu.int/comm/development/body/legislation/docs/council_statement.pdf EC Country Strategy Paper India.* 10 September 2002. At *http://ec.europa.eu/comm/external_relations/india/csp/02_06en.pdf*

GoI (2004). EC Communication titled *An EU-India Strategic Partnership: India's Response.* At *http://meaindia.nic.in/onmouse/EU-Indian.pdf*

Reports

Consortium Eva-EU c/o NCG (2002). *Evaluation of Council Regulation N.443/92 on Cooperation between the EC and ALA countries, Final Report.* May. At *http://ec.europa.eu/comm/europeaid/evaluation/reports/ala/951614.pdf*

ADE (2002). *Clarifying the Definitions of EC Economic Cooperation with Third Countries.* At *http://web.particip.de/pac-rep/voletb/docs/axe1/951636.pdf*

Asian Development Bank (2006). *The Millennium Development Goals: Progress in Asia and the Pacific.* At *http://www.adb.org/Documents/Books/MDG-Asia-Pacific/default.asp*

Development Strategies Consultancy (2006). *EU Donor Atlas Volume I, Mapping Official Development Assistance.* February. At *http://ec.europa.eu/comm/development/body/publications/docs/eu_donor_atlas_2006.pdf*

Other

Jaffrelot, Christophe (2006). *India and the European Union: The Charade of a Strategic Partnership.* CERI-Sciences-Po, Archives. At *http://www.ceri-sciencespo.com/archive/mars06/art_cj.pdf*

2

Comparisons between Indo-US Relations and India-EU Relations

Political and Economic Ramifications

SATEESH KULKARNI

Summary

The relationship between India and the US has reached a stage, which one may term as 'definitive'. There have been visible signs of a newfound confidence that is clearly different from the tentative 'highs' that relations had reached in the past. Trade will be a big driver in cementing these relations and political ideologies will no longer be influenced by rigid agendas.

Similarly, the EU-India relations have now moved to higher and firmer grounds. It has also moved onto a broader spectrum encompassing, apart from trade and politics, cooperation in the cultural, educational and social frameworks.

This paper looks at these changing dimensions and how the world canvas would look like in the years to come.

India-US Relations

Background

Why have India and the US not enjoyed long-term stable bilateral ties expected of two ideologically similar nations? This is a complex question and hinges on a variety of factors—economic national interests, geo-strategic compulsions and perceptions of the US State Department and the Pentagon. In spite of synergies between the two nations—respect for democracy, human rights and individual liberty, commitment to the rule of law, and market economy—the historical course of India-US relations has been guided by extraneous factors such as Pakistan, politics in the Middle East and Soviet influence in the region. Compulsions of Cold War politics led the US to view India from a prism that also had the former Soviet Union and Pakistan in focus. With the end of the Cold War and the collapse of the Soviet Union, Pakistan and China formed the context for India-assessment. After independence, India took the initiative in developing the Non-Aligned Movement which subscribed to the policy of maintaining equidistance from both the USA and the USSR. Even though it chose not to join any of the power blocks, its inclination towards the Soviet Union was apparent. Specifically after the India-China War (1961) and the Indo-Pak war (1965), where Soviet support was apparent, India made considerable change in its foreign policies and attempted to pursue even-handed economic and military relations with the Soviet Union. In 1971, India entered into a 20 year friendship treaty with the erstwhile USSR. This had an adverse effect on the Indo-US relationship with growing suspicions between both the countries. At the same time, in an apparent attempt to counter growing Soviet influence in the subcontinent, the US tilt towards Pakistan became more pronounced. However, a lot has changed since the end of the Cold War era. India-US relations have improved dramatically. This has largely been fostered by the fact that both the countries are viewing the relationship with more maturity and the fact that both the US and India are democracies and have a large and growing trade relationship.

Evolution of the Political Relationship

During the Gulf War, the economy of India went through an extremely difficult phase. The Government of India liberalised the Indian economy. After the break up of the Soviet Union, India started looking for new allies and tried improving diplomatic relations with the members of NATO particularly the United States, Canada, France and Germany.

In the mid-1990s, India tried to attract world attention towards Pakistan backed terrorism in Kashmir. The Kargil War in 1996 proved to the world that Indian protests of over-the-border infiltration and Pakistan backed terrorism over the years were not a figment of the imagination. This war resulted in a major diplomatic victory for India. The United States and the European Union recognised the fact that the Pakistani military had illegally infiltrated Indian territory and pressurised Pakistan to withdraw from Kargil. Several anti-India terrorist groups based in Pakistan were labelled as terrorist groups by the United States and the European Union.

In 1998, India tested nuclear weapons (usually mentioned as Pokhran-II) which resulted in several US, Japanese and European sanctions on India. The United States imposed economic sanctions in response to India's nuclear tests in May 1998 which led to a deterioration in relations between the two countries. The United States encouraged India to sign the Comprehensive Test Ban Treaty ('CTBT') and also called for restraint in missile and nuclear testing and deployment by both India and Pakistan. However the non-proliferation dialogue initiated after the 1998 nuclear tests helped in taking the relationship ahead.

After the end of the Cold War, and the collapse of the so-called Soviet power bloc, suspicion and animosity have given way to a degree of trust and it was imperative that cooperation would be a key word between the two.

In 2002, the then US ambassador to India, Robert Blackwill used the metaphor "flat as a *chapatti*" (unleavened Indian bread) to describe the fact that bilateral trade between the two countries volumes still lack critical mass. Blackwill also said that with a billion-plus population, India's two-way trade with the US is still less than that of Ireland, with a population of only four million. Some of the problems that the Americans faced at different times include the one-step forward, two-steps-back nature of India's economic reforms since the early 1990s. There was also the perception that the rule of law in India to protect IPR is weak, despite the fact that Indian courts often deliver swift justice in the case of infringements in trademarks.

Both India and the US have realised that it is mutually beneficial to develop the relationship both in trade and politically. There are many reasons why the US, wants to build India into a world power. —one of them being the rich and powerful million-strong Indian-American community that is starting to flex its muscles to gain electoral and political influence. However, geopolitical reasons are by far the most important. The Americans have realised that India is the world's largest democracy with a huge buying power. Also, a strong and vibrant India could easily become the US supporter in the war against terrorism and a restraint on China's ambitions in the sub-continent. This has been President Bush's totally radical strategy in South Asia.

The Present Equation

The US and India share a six decade history of bilateral relationship and over the years, the US has given India its due importance in the international arena. However, India and the United States have traditionally had a 'blow hot-blow cold' relationship. The political relations have no doubt warmed ever since the Clinton era as compared to the stand-offish and distant attitude of the Cold War period. However, one finds that American foreign policy advisors of successive governments framed their India policy with the narrow vision of the Cold War outlook. Every nation was either for the US or against them and had a Soviet tilt. This was the attitude they projected when they ought to have broadened their horizon and evolved a customised and country-specific policy for India. The Indian policy makers too refused to take advantage of their enormous goodwill in America and only reacted within the limited and perhaps inflexible framework and sensibilities of the non-aligned movement without bothering about the implications of a changed world order.

"US and Them"—The Pakistan Paradox

Condoleeza Rice's statement that the US would like to see/help India grow into a super power warmed the hearts of the Indian government. The Indian government felt that at least they had managed to get the kind of respect that they deserved as the leading nation in south Asia. For just that statement, their whole outlook towards America changed and they were willing to forgive the Americans for their pro-Pakistan stance. In fact, even the announcement made by President Bush on the sale of F-16 fighters to Pakistan did not evoke the kind of angry response from the Indian side as usual!

On the flip side, India has wholeheartedly supported the US on various critical issues including its war against terror in Afghanistan and the Middle East and against Iran for its non-compliance with the non-proliferation treaty in 2005. The US while appreciating India's point of view regarding Pakistan sponsored terrorism has done little concrete besides offering pious platitudes that do nothing to ease the situation. In fact, the view commonly held in India has been that while India gets the rhetoric, the Pakistanis get the F-16 fighter jets!

Economic Dimension of Indo-US Relations

Although power and security still constitute the nuclei of foreign policy in all countries, the emphasis on economic aspects has assumed greater significance. The emergence of a global economy, characterised by growth in world trade and the spread of foreign investments in international markets, has clearly changed the paradigm governing relations between states.

Beyond all these strategic geopolitical factors are the economic considerations that are getting prominence in taking relations between the two countries further. Economic reforms introduced since 1991 have radically changed the course of the Indian economy and led to its gradual integration with the global economy. Benefits of the reform process are visible in the form of better growth rates, higher investment and trade flows and accelerated decline in income poverty.

The effects of these reforms on trade and investment relations with the United States have been profound. The USA is the largest investing country in India and US investments cover almost every sector in India, which is open for private participants.

India-US economic relations have to be examined from two perspectives—the Indo-American trade relations and US foreign direct investments in India. The US has emerged as the largest trading partner and most favourite export destination. The two-way trade between India and the US increased to $12.79 billion in 1999—a more than 100 per cent increase since 1992. In January-May 2000, India's exports to the US totalled $4.53 billion, while imports stood at $1.53 billion resulting in a positive trade balance of $3 billion. Indo-US bilateral trade during January-May'06 amounted to $26.8 bn and the aim is to take this to $60 bn within the next three years. Bilateral trade between the two countries has shown a quantum jump of nearly

30 per cent in 2005-06 from 25 per cent in the preceding year. Trade volume is expected to reach USD 30 billion in 2006-07.

The US continues to be the leading investor in India in terms of foreign direct investment (FDI), approvals, actual inflows and portfolio investment. Of the total FDI of $60 billion that India received between 1991 and May 2000, approvals from the US constituted $13 billion. If Euro issues and NRI investments are excluded, then the US accounts for 22 per cent of the total FDI commitments made to India in this period. However, US' total trade turnover with India is less than 1 per cent of its global trade. India is ranked 23rd among countries exporting to the US, and is yet to become its favourite FDI destination.

While India appreciates the slowly increasing FDI that is coming into the country from the US which has been forthcoming in critical sectors, in high tech areas, quality standards and areas of corporate governance, it has so much to offer by way of its burgeoning middle class with a hefty buying power, a relatively young and educated workforce and a mature legal system apart from local suzerainty.

The developing Indian economy holds much promise for both countries. With growth reaching double digits, the Indian economic miracle could become the basis for closer relations between the two countries. With economic strength will come the justification for a strategic partnership between both countries. The Indian policy makers initiated economic reforms and liberalisation in an effort to globalise the economy. However, it needs to be realised that this process of globalisation cannot survive in a vacuum. India will need to partner other similar economies to profit from the steps that are being taken. In such a world, it is imperative that India and the US mutually assist and collaborate to take this process of strategic and economic cooperation forward.

The US-China-India triangle

Though American investments in China are 10 times that in India, recent trends show a drop. During 2002 to 2005, US investment in China dropped by over 43 per cent. In contrast, US investment in India zoomed 68 per cent. In 2005, US investments in China totalled $3.06 billion compared to $0.47 billion in India. Two-thirds of the US investment in China is in the manufacturing sector. In 2004, transport and electrical equipment accounted for 44.6 per cent of the US investments in China. Ironically, these investments boomeranged on the US. Foreign firms in China, including American ones, became exporters to the US, leading to a yawning trade deficit and raising fears of unemployment in the US.

India's Attraction

In contrast to FDI in China, the bulk of US investment in India flowed into computer software and related areas, followed by consultancy/service sectors. Also, US investors did not face problems in India over protection of intellectual propriety rights (IPR), as they did in China. India has a product patent regime in place, and its regulations are WTO compatible.

The US is one of the largest foreign direct investors in India. This is proved by the fact that the stock of actual FDI inflow increased from a paltry US $11.3 million in 1991 to US $4856 million as on September 2005, recording an increase at a compound rate of 57.5 per cent per annum. FDI inflows from US constitute about 11 per cent of total actual FDI inflows into India.

Figure 2.1

India: Share of Top Investing Countries FDI Inflows (Aug. 1991 to Sept. 2005)

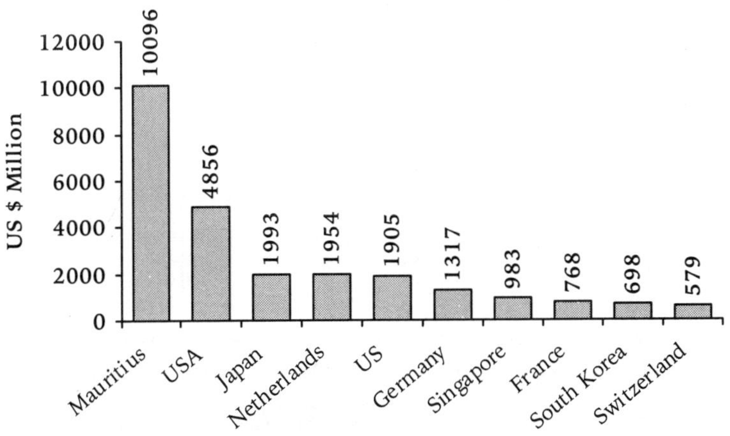

Source: Dept. of Industrial Policy and Promotion, Ministry of Commerce, Government of India.

India's investments in the US are picking up. The US is also India's largest trading partner. By 2003, India became the 24th largest export destination for the US. In terms of exports to the US, India now ranks as the eighteenth largest country. And the US faces a trade deficit with India.

Since 2000, the two countries have been making efforts to strengthen the institutional structure of bilateral economic relations by means of the "India-US Economic Dialogue" that aims at deepening the Indo-American partnership through regular dialogue and engagement.

This effort has had an apparent positive impact on the bilateral trade. The bilateral trade in goods forecast for the financial year 2005-2006 is supposed to exceed $30 billion for the first time, putting the two countries well on the way towards achieving the goal—endorsed in early 2006 by President Bush and Indian PM Manmohan Singh—of doubling bilateral trade in three years.

These deliberations also resulted in some important commercial milestones in 2006, starting from Air India's $10 bn purchase of 68 Boeing Aircraft to IBM's announcement of a major investment in India. Another important event was the positive response of Indian business towards the largest ever US trade delegation to visit India consisting of over 180 companies, the largest ever US delegation to any country.

Figure 2.2

India's Trade with US, Balance

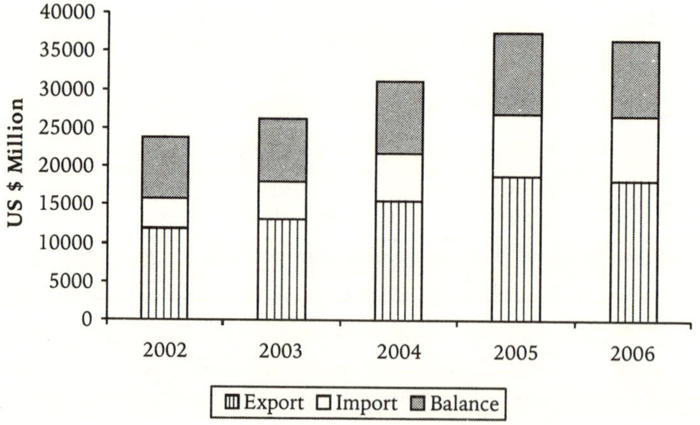

Source: Dept. of Industrial Policy and Promotion, Ministry of Commerce, Government of India.

In a purely bilateral context, Indo-US economic relations have grown in the last five decades. But what holds promise for a better future is the growing American interest in India's policy of economic liberalisation. A basic reality about India is that it is a large and growing economy offering new business and investment opportunities to the world. Although China, Japan, and the European Union (EU) remain the biggest markets for American products and services, the big emerging market in India—sixth largest in the world in terms of Purchasing Power Parity (PPP), a sophisticated market-economy infrastructure, stable parliamentary democracy with an independent judiciary, and a large reservoir of technical and managerial manpower—holds greater possibilities of large incremental gains in exports.

One of the greatest success stories of the Indo-American relationship which made business sense and was the reason why the relationship came back on an even keel was the BPO story. Although 'American companies outsourcing their work to India' phenomenon initially met with resistance and ire in the US, the economic benefits to the economy made strong business sense. Many US corporations cutback on their internal workforce and outsourced work to captive units or independent third-party suppliers in India. This has raised hackles all around as it meant the loss of existing jobs while increasing employment at offshore locations in India. It also made the Indian BPO success story a cause for concern in the US.

However, President Bush lent his support by terming outsourcing an effective and competitive means for American companies to foray into the global market. And it is indeed a winning proposition for both countries. The operating costs of a BPO outfit in India have been calculated to be a mere 20 per cent of those in America. The Indian BPO industry currently employs over 900,000 people and is expected to employ 2 million people by 2008 The US is one of the largest clients of the BPO industry in India. Anywhere from 50 per cent to 70 per cent of all Fortune 500 companies are already outsourcing to India, and, according to a research report, the amount of work done there for US companies is expected to more than double this year. A large pool of highly qualified technical manpower, improved infrastructure, advantage of a differential time zone and English speaking skills have made India an attractive destination for BPO work.

Future Prospects

The changing dimensions of this newfound confidence between the two countries is now visible in areas perhaps not even imaginable a decade back.

In December 2006, the US Congress by an overwhelming majority, passed a law allowing New Delhi to buy US nuclear reactors and fuel for the first time in 30 years, the development has been heralded as a big step towards the initiation of a new era of strategic partnership that has been built over the ruins of years of detachment between the two countries, triggered by Cold War politics. The landmark agreement between India and the US on civil nuclear cooperation fulfills many objectives. America develops a good working relationship with India, which is increasingly becoming important internationally, as well as manages to keep an unobtrusive eye on the Indian nuclear programme without seeming to step on Indian toes. India too benefits as it has continued access to nuclear fuel and technology and can keep its nuclear programme running in the face of constant threats over its borders from China and Pakistan. The US too gets to increase its influence over the geopolitically sensitive region of Asia. This agreement will help in deepening Indian integration with key international institutions such as the Nuclear Suppliers Group (NSG), and the International Atomic Energy Agency (IAEA). Under this new civil nuclear agreement, India has agreed to separate its civilian and military programmes and to put two-thirds of its existing reactors, and 65 per cent of its generating power, under permanent safeguards with international verification, in reciprocation of which the United States will supply nuclear fuel and technology to India. This is very vital for India, because India plans to use nuclear energy as the source of all its future power requirements and over the past few years this programme has been hampered due to a lack of nuclear fuel and technology.

Nuclear energy, which at present accounts for only about three per cent of India's total electricity generation will answer to a great extent India's need for power for its boomimg economy, which would otherwise be burdened by the expense on imported oil and fast depleting reserves of coal. This would allow the United States to bring

India under IAEA inspection and control and solve India's technology and energy issues to a great extent. The agreement seems to be a win-win situation for both countries and has moved the relationship to a higher level that ever before. Equally, the conclusion of a 10-year framework agreement on defence cooperation during the then Defence Minister Pranab Mukherjee's visit to Washington in June 2005 is further evidence of the expanding scope of military cooperation with the US.

These have been heralded as a big step towards the initiation of a new era of strategic partnership. With new realities replacing old ones, the United States faces myriad challenges. In its effort to maintain supremacy in a world that is witnessing the rise of other major powers, Washington is relentlessly following a policy of 'engagement'. The February 2006 Quadrennial Defence Review (which sets the defence agenda of the US administration every four to five years), in keeping with this US objective, very appropriately submits that, "building partnership capacity invigorates US efforts and acknowledges that future challenges can be met only through the integrated use of all of the instruments of national power and through the relevant contributions of their international partners." With this serving as the backdrop, the United States is attempting to carve out a strategic partnership with India in order to remain engaged with the region as a whole.

This wooing of India is seen as the US move to counter a rising China in Asia. Many see a turning point in the aftermath of the US invasion of Afghanistan. Since China went slow in extending military support to Pakistan, the tension on the Indo-Pak border eased. China has also decided to strengthen economic relations with India; in a very short while, it has emerged as India's second largest trading partner. To contain the China factor, the US had to come closer to India. During the Clinton era, China was given much more importance and India's nuclear programme was slowed to a great extent, Bush took the measured view that improving relations with India would get him greater political as well as economic mileage along with playing a balancing act with China. In the present context, there is a convergence of interest in keeping a wary eye on Chinese policies and actions.

In today's circumstances, the nuclear deal has assumed a symbolic importance to signify the changed relationship. The major test for the two countries lies ahead. Although compromises are in the very nature of a mutually beneficial relationship, there are red lines that cannot be crossed.

India-EU Relations: Changing Dimensions

Indo EU relations can be traced back to the early 1960s. It was the time when India chose to be one of the few countries that established diplomatic relations with the erstwhile European Economic Community (EEC). There have been distinct phases in this journey that have cemented this relationship. The 'milestones' could be clearly seen: the 1993 Joint Political Statement, the 1994 EU India Cooperation Agreement; the first India EU Summit in Lisbon in 2000, which in many ways could be termed as the watershed in the evolving relationship that has gone well beyond being just a trade relationship. The years following this, witnessed Summit level interactions and the forging of mature ties based on mutual understanding and trust.

The Current Status

The European Union's 25-member states combined represent the world's largest economy by GDP, the seventh largest territory in the world by area and the third largest by population. The EU is India's largest trading partner accounting for about 22 per cent of India's global trade. The India-EU relationship started essentially as a partnership for development and economic cooperation. However, it has evolved over the years to a stage where both sides have decided to elevate their engagement to the level of a formal strategic partnership spanning all aspects—political, cultural, social and economic.

Europe with nearly 370 million citizens, a high purchasing power and a common currency is also India's largest potential market. Yet, India-EU relations have not realised their true potential expected of two economic powers. However, the two share several common features from democratic traditions and an independent judiciary to a rich cultural diversity and the commitment to economic progress, community values and social development.

Relations between India and the EU, encompassing diverse areas including energy, trade, science and technology, have been growing ever since the strategic partnership was launched at the India-EU summit in The Hague. Europe is also a growing market for Indian investment. Since 2000, Indian companies have invested more than $10 billion in Europe. They have made a number of impressive inroads into the EU market, of which the Mittal Steel acquisition of Arcelor was only the most striking. Indian foreign investment to the EU has increased five-fold in the last 10 years.

The Changing Relationships

However, the evolving of the EU from an economic community to a union of states looking to formulate a common foreign and security policy started getting reflected in its relationship with India. Efforts to formulate and bring forward a long-term strategic partnership with intensified political involvement are becoming apparent.

The Joint Political Statement signed in 1993 can be seen as the milestone for initiation of a broader political dialogue between the EU and India. The statement suggested annual ministerial meetings between the two. The next step was the cooperation agreement signed in 1994 that envisaged taking bilateral relations beyond the realms of trade and economic cooperation. The agreement instructed setting up of an EC India Joint Commission, a central guardian mechanism to oversee and inspire the entire range of cooperation activities between India and the EC. Three separate sub-commissions, on trade; economic cooperation; development cooperation, cover a more detailed agenda and report directly to the Joint Commission. There have been serious implementations of these decisions from both the sides with deliberations on these issues.

India also imposes a number of non-tariff barriers in the form of quantitative restrictions, import licensing, mandatory testing and certification for a large number of products, as well as complicated and lengthy customs procedures. Overall India's high tariff levels remain a genuine problem for European industry. Tariff reductions and in particular bindings on a much lower level are an important goal of the multilateral negotiations.

Under the National Indicative Programme for India 2002-2003, the EU has in the Trade and Investment Development Programme earmarked €14 million to assist India in better integrating into the world economy and promoting bilateral trade. Specific projects aimed at helping India meet EU sanitary and phytosanitary requirements, deal with issues related to intellectual property rights and customs procedures, and facilitate investment in India. The EU also funds trade related projects under the Asia Trust Fund and the Asia Invest Programmes.

The ongoing Free Trade Agreement (FTA) covers not just trade in goods, but also services and investments. While India is interested in having greater access for its professionals in the EU market, the European Union wants India to lower duties on industrial goods. It will also see the signing of an "action plan" that will chart out a way forward for political, trade and investment, economic, cultural, and academic relations. Such an action plan will also work against terrorism and build up a security dialogue. Besides, it will endeavour to meet common environmental challenges by strengthening two way exchanges in alternate fuel technologies. India-EU FTA marks a willing urge to forge "Strategic Partnership" and cooperate in areas such as space and energy. The agreement will confirm India as a global player and bring New Delhi into an elite club of countries that includes the US, Canada, Russia and Japan. India's cooperation in the fusion energy project and renewed flexibility on the part of the EU, to give India access to encryption codes for military grade end has emerged as an important area of cooperation. New Delhi also stands to gain in certain other fields such as textiles and biotechnology.

According to the Indian Commerce Minister, "a free trade accord between India and the European union will help in breaking the current impasse in the World Trade Organization." FTAs are "building blocks" of a multilateral global order. These initiatives will help break the impasse in the WTO. New Delhi is certainly looking for investments, but it is also an investor. The issue of lowering duties on wines and spirits imported from EU countries has emerged as a major area of contention. The EU is asking India to open up its market to agricultural products like wine. Concerns are also increasing on revenue and reciprocity. The EU also supported India's demand for safeguarding the interests of its farmers. The EU also favoured the protection of Indian agriculture through the mechanism of Special Products Scheme (SPS), and pointed out that SPS aims at ensuring the livelihood of subsistence farmers. He accepted that, highly subsidised farm products harm the interest of developing countries like India. The EU wants New Delhi to grant greater access in the information technology (IT) sector. It held that, India stands to gain by liberalising trade and services, and by opening up its market in sectors such as biotechnology, agriculture etc.

Prospects

The cornerstone of the India-EU relationship lies in trade and investment. Foreign direct investment (FDI) remains a critical element for the development of all sectors of the Indian economy. The top sectors attracting FDI from the EU are fuels (power and oil refinery), telecommunications, transportation industries, chemicals (other than fertilisers) and electrical equipments, including computers software. EU countries such as the UK, Germany, France, Italy, the Netherlands, Belgium and Sweden are among the leading foreign investors in India.

There is no doubt that there is enormous room for improvement. While the EU is aiming at revitalising and sustaining its developed economy, India is striving to become a developed economy within 20 years. These two processes have great synergy, and that is why there is need to explore a strategic relationship. The bold reforms undertaken by the Union government will give a boost to economic growth in India and to trade relations with European countries.

EU-India trade has grown impressively over the years, from €4.4 billion in 1980 to €40 billion in 2005. Trade with the EU represents more than 20 per cent of Indian's exports and imports and the EU thus as a bloc is India's largest trading partner. In goods and services, the EU is India's largest trading partner which accounted for 21.1 per cent of India's exports and imports in 2005. India ranks as EU's 10th trading partner accounting for 1.8 per cent of the EU exports and imports. In 2005, EU imports from India amounted to €18.9 billion (covering mainly textiles/clothing, agricultural products and chemicals) while EU exports to India amounted to €21.1 billion (covering mostly machinery and chemical products). During 2005 EU-

India trade increased by 20.3 per cent and has increased with an annual average of 11.1 per cent between 2001 and 2005.

The EU is also India's largest source of foreign direct investment. However, India accounts for just 1.8 per cent of total EU trade. India attracts only 0.3 per cent of the EU's world-wide investments.

EU and India in WTO

India is one of the founding members of both GATT and the WTO. Although India is critical of the implications of the results of the Uruguay Round for developing countries and is sceptical of the broad agenda of the current round of multilateral negotiations (Doha Round), it is clearly committed to advancing the multilateral trading system.

In the WTO, too, the EU considers itself to be a 'natural ally' of India despite sharp differences over farm subsidy policies as well as on issues relating to market access. New Delhi and Brussels are increasingly having consultations before meetings on key issues. No doubt, unlike in the political arena, there are much sharper exchanges on WTO matters, largely because India is not only a major player but also an important member of major groupings such as the Group of 20 developing countries and the Group of 33. The interests of these groups are virtually diametrically opposite to that of the EU and the US, though negotiations are continuing in a bid to reach some form of agreement by the Hong Kong ministerial conference in December.

What has caused concern in the EU is India's increasing use of anti-dumping legislation and the fact that it has ruled against the EU in 27 cases since 1999—far more than any other exporter. However, New Delhi's contention in this direction is that, the EU is using non tariff barriers to block imports from India, such as shrimps and herbal medicines. The Indian exporters face a large number of non tariff barriers in the EU market. Given its developing country status, India's exports to the EU benefit from reduced tariffs under the EU Generalised System of Preferences. India is the largest beneficiary of this scheme with preferences covering imports of a value of €8bn during 2005. In sharp contrast to this Indian exporters have had to suffer at the hands of European agencies, due to the rejection of their consignments of food and agricultural products on health and safety grounds. According to a European Commerce Ministry estimate, Indian exporters have lost business worth Rs 10 billion due to rejection of goods and their subsequent dumping during 2005-06.

Hopefully, such an agreement will prove fruitful for both the EU and India and encourage positive competition, specialisation and drive down prices for consumers by increasing economic efficiency. It is also hoped that this will contribute to economic development and growth and enhance technological capability.

EU and the Indo-US N-deal

The EU has chosen to remain non-committal on the issue of the Indo-US Nuclear deal, saying it understood India's increasing energy needs. However it gave no commitment on supporting the Indo-US civilian nuclear deal. The 25-member European Union is making efforts to evolve a common policy on the issue. However the Union is of the view that the debates on the India-United States nuclear deal, should address the basic issue of non-proliferation. The European Parliament supports India's quest for civilian nuclear energy, but wants it to sign the Nuclear Non-Proliferation Treaty (NPT) to speed up international civilian nuclear cooperation.

Britain and France have come out strongly in support of the India-US civilian nuclear deal, while Germany has shown signs of softening on the issue, indicating that it may support India in the powerful Nuclear Suppliers Group. But the Nordic countries, including Finland, which holds the current rotating presidency of the EU, have expressed their anxieties about countries like India, that are seeking global civilian nuclear commerce without signing the NPT.

Conclusion

Any way one looks at it, India-EU economic relations look very positive and are expected to only improve over time. This is indeed what must be concluded from the official statements issued after the seventh India-EU summit meeting held in Helsinki last year. A significant point of the meeting was the agreement to "commence negotiations on a broad-based Trade and Investment Agreement between India and the European Union covering over 90 per cent of tariff lines and trade volume."

There is no doubt that, as the Indian Prime Minister said, that such an accord would constitute a "very significant step that would build on the complementarities in the trade flows between the two sides whereby reduction in tariffs over a period of time will be a win-win situation for both." This would be especially true for India because the EU is its largest trading partner and the most important source of investment flows. But having said this, it would only be proper to state that though the intention is noble, implementation may be problematic. Going by reports on the negotiations that led up to the agreement to begin talks on a broader economic accord between the two sides, it is clear that Brussels is still entrenched in its views on subjects such as non-tariff barriers to trade, which are a serious obstacle to increasing Indian exports to the EU. India's basic strategy would be to thrash out an agreement that incorporates as many of the WTO trade guidelines as possible, an initiative which Brussels may not prefer, in view of the fact that such 'concessions' to a country like India would have the effect of weakening its overall bargaining position at the WTO negotiating table.

Although there may appear to be speed breakers ahead and the road may not appear smooth, the EU objective appears to be to conclude a free trade agreement with India, which would result in greater economic benefits for Brussels given the huge Indian market, instead of a wider trade and investment agreement including services, which would be more productive for New Delhi, given the growing international stature of the software and knowledge-based services sector. However, it must be adequately impressed upon Brussels that with appropriate safeguards built in, the broader agreement could turn out to be valuable to the EU too. It remains to be seen as to what extent Brussels will finally give in to New Delhi's demands on this and other issues.

3

India and China

Cooperation, Competition and Some Repercussions on the Western World

C. RAJA MOHAN and KLAUS JULIAN VOLL

After decades of tensions and deep mutual mistrust, India and China have sought to construct a normal and cooperative relationship over the last few years. The visit of President Hu Jintao—only the second by a Chinese President in the last six decades—between the 20th and 23rd of November 2006 to Delhi and Mumbai marked an important step in the evolution of the envisaged 'strategic relationship' between these two emerging Asian powers on the world scene.

For a long time, China's leaders wrote off India as inconsequential, but have been repeatedly surprised by New Delhi in recent years—the nuclear tests in 1998, New Delhi's big power diplomacy that followed, India's economic rejuvenation and its political rise on the world stage. Today Sino-Indian relations are in their most productive phase since the last 60 years. Military tensions on the border have long ceased and there is enduring peace and tranquility. The two countries have already agreed on a set of principles to resolve the long-standing boundary dispute and both sides are formally committed to an early and final settlement. The long festering dispute over Sikkim has already been settled during 2003-2005. The idea of a free trade treaty or comprehensive economic cooperation between the two countries is beginning to gain ground. More frequent political contacts at the highest levels, like the agreed Annual Summit between China and India and a hotline between the two Foreign Ministers—both a result of Hu's visit—will facilitate a better cooperation in future.

Yet there is also the concern that China's weight and influence in the world and the region have grown rapidly in recent years. On the other hand, "Hu's visit took place in the backdrop of an international milieu that has changed remarkably in China's favour."[1] Despite the renewed US influence in the Sub-continent, China has become a powerful player in its own right in South Asia. Having distanced itself somewhat from the Sub-continent after the Soviet withdrawal from Afghanistan at the end of 1980s, the US is back in the Sub-continent with a bang, thanks to the dramatic events of September 11, 2001. Since then it has revived military and economic cooperation with Pakistan and simultaneously defined a new framework for strategic partnership with India."[2] This new US activism in the Sub-continent, however, has not stopped China from raising its own political profile in the region. Security analyst Brahma Chellaney, who is critical *vis-à-vis* many aspects of India's foreign policy and author of the book *Asian Juggernaut: The Rise of China, India and Japan,*[3] observes, "Gwadar (a port built by the Chinese close to the Persian Gulf) epitomizes the way China is quietly but determinedly encroaching on India's strategic backyard by assembling a "string of pearls" in the form of ports, listening posts and naval agreements stretching from Pakistan and Sri Lanka to Bangladesh and Burma. Having stepped up direct and surrogate pressure on India's north, China is now threatening to challenge the dominant Indian role in the Indian Ocean."[4] Therefore, Hu Jintao's visit to India—and afterwards to Pakistan (see Section 5)—marks the emergence of a new role for Beijing in the political and economic evolution of the Sub-continent.

The Western World—especially Europe—should systematically take note of these new developments, including the simultaneous partnership and rivalry between New Delhi and Beijing, the growing economic dynamism in the Sub-continent and its integration into East Asia, and the rapidly altering geopolitical dynamics in the context of

1. Sudarshan, V. (2006). "Who Goes There? Friend or foe... India Assesses What China Means for its Own Place in Asia", *The Outlook*. November 27. p.33
2. Mohan, C. Raja (2006). *Impossible Allies: Nuclear India, United States and the Global Order.* New Delhi: India Research Press.
3. Chellaney, Brahma (2006). *Asian Juggernaut: The Rise of China, India and Japan*. New Delhi: Harper Collins and India Today Group.
4. Chellaney, Brahma (2006). "Imperial China", *The Hindustan Times*. October 30. p.8

South Asia. Will the Western world, the United States of America and especially Europe, remain a silent spectator?

The USA, after their intensive engagement with New Delhi since Clinton's path-breaking visit in India in 2000 and particularly since the nuclear deal under the Bush administration in 2005, is definitely a highly interested party. The China factor has become an important component of US policy towards India. But what about Germany, France and England or Europe as a whole? Would they be happy to remain well-informed spectators or even idle fence-sitters amidst what could be a consequential triangular power play between India, China, and the US? What indeed are the European interests in the emerging Asian balance of power and how should it protect them? The paper hopes to provide some answers to these questions.

Between Distrust and a New Beginning[5]

After the bonhomie ("*Hindi Chini Bhai Bhai*") in the 1950's between China and India[6], their short border war led to a humiliating defeat for India in 1962 and to a unilateral Chinese declaration of a cease-fire. This defeat inflicted a lasting trauma on the Indian nation, especially its political and military elite. China could, so it seemed, never be trusted.[7]

It took 26 years before India sought to break the mould of Sino-Indian relations. In 1988, the late Prime Minister Rajiv Gandhi had visited China. His initiative saw decisions to pursue renewed negotiations on the boundary dispute and a steady normalisation of bilateral relations. In the 1990s high level exchanges continued with Prime Minister P.V. Narasimha Rao traveling to Beijing in 1993 and Chinese President Jiang Zemin visiting India in 1996.[8]

---

5. See "Time-Table of India-China Relations".

6. Indo-Chinese Treaty of 1954 with its five principles (Panchsheel), which amongst others recognised the mutual territorial integrity and sovereignty.

7. This is till date also the essence of the arguments of the well-informed P. Stobdan, the new Director, Centre for Strategic and Regional Studies (CSRS), University of Jammu. "Tackling the Mandarins". *The Hindustan Times*. November 16, 2006. p.10 and "Never Trust China". *Outlook*. November 27, 2006. p.44

8. Agreement on the Maintainance of Peace and Tranquility in Border Areas along the Line of Actual Control (LAC), Beijing 1993.

In early 1998, George Fernandes, the then Defence Minister, seemed to disrupt the wary rapproachement between the two nations when he declared in his Krishna Menon[9] Memorial Lecture, the People's Republic of China as "India's enemy (adversary) Number One." A prominent politician privately criticised him for going public, yet added, "George has only said what all of us think." India's nuclear tests in May 1998, New Delhi's decision to cite the China threat as one of the reasons and the harsh Chinese reaction once again threatened to derail the relationship. The two countries, however, quickly sought to pick up the pieces.

Ironically, the same George Fernandes, an erstwhile Socialist and one of India's most experienced politicians, traveled later as Defence Minister to China and prepared the landmark visit of the then Prime Minister Atal Bihari Vajpayee in 2003, which led to India's *de facto* recognition of Tibet as a part of China. But still at the turn of the century George Fernandes complained about the slow progress in the then ongoing meetings about the border problems.[10]

India's status as a nuclear power and the rapidly changing international equations after 9/11 with a marked presence of the United States in South Asia, including the new quality in India-US relations, led obviously to a rethinking in Beijing's strategy *vis-à-vis* India. In 2001, Li Peng, then No. 3 in the Chinese power structure, paved the way for a new quality in India-China relations,[11] leading to a whole sequence of high-level interactions till date.

Distrust not only amongst the elites but also amongst the general populace is definitely still there on both sides, although the peaceful co-existence between these two great Asian civilisations over thousands of years is increasingly stressed in public speeches. Brahma Chellaney holds "the negative stereotyping of India in Chinese school

---

9. Krishna Menon, a very close confidante of India's first Prime Minister Jawaharlal Nehru, had to resign after the defeat in the 1962 to war.

10. "They (the Chinese) are mocking us."

11. Voll, Klaus (2006). "Tete à Tete between the Chinese Dragon and the Indian Elephant: Li Peng in India, 2001", in Voll, Klaus and Doreen Beierlein (eds.), *Rising India – Europe's Partner? Foreign and Security Policy, Politics, Economics, Human Rights and Social Issues, Media, Civil Society and Intercultural Dimensions*. Berlin: Berlin Studies in International Politics and Societies and New Delhi: Mosaic Books. pp.35-47.

textbooks" as partly responsible.[12] On the other side, about 60 per cent of educated Indians—readers of at least one English or vernacular daily—see in China less a threat than an opportunity and an important ally on global issues. "Although about 30 per cent still view China as India's biggest enemy, it is significant that double that number believes it is a good friend and a potential ally. Nearly 17 per cent see China as India's best friend in today's world. That the US and Russia are allies to an equal degree (30 per cent each) could be interpreted as a sign of reorientation of worldviews because such parity would have been inconceivable during the Cold War or in pre-reform years."[13]

Political and Nuclear Cooperation

Perhaps it is more than a rhetorical statement, when it is said that both China and India do no longer see each other as rivals in the evolving International System, that they intend to concede to each other sufficient space and do envisage cooperation in various fields. During his visit to New Delhi, Hu Jintao said, "Sino-Indian relation has gone beyond bilateral context and acquired global dimension–as two fastest growing economies in the world, India and China need to participate in global issues from energy security, environment protection, cross-border violence and a host of other issues."[14]

In an address to the Indian people, the visiting Chinese President envisaged the future relations on a higher plane, consisting of such elements like building trust, creating institutional connections, a fast resolution of the boundary issues, improved economic relations, student exchange and expansion of tourism as well as increased multi-lateral cooperation.

After his interaction with Prime Minister Dr. Manmohan Singh, Hu Jintao spoke of a "new historic beginning" for India and China and

12. "Chinese Don't Trust Indians". Stereotyping of India in Textbooks to Blame: Survey. *The Times of India*, November 12, 2006. p.8

13. Mudgal, Vipul (2006). "Rooting for Peace (based on an exclusive nationwide HT Survey)", in *India Rising: Hindustan Times Leadership Supplement*. November 17. New Delhi.

14. Speech at the Indian Council of World Affairs, quoted in Bhattacherjee, Kallol (2006). "Whooping it up. Chinese President Hu Jintao plays 'Big Boy Diplomacy' in Delhi". *The Week*, December 3. pp.34-35

that the "establishment of strategic partnership with India is a strategic choice exercised by China, (and was) not a political expedient."[15]

Thirteen agreements on trade, agriculture and education were signed during President Hu's visit. The opening of a Chinese Consulate in Kolkata[16] gives China access also to Northeast India whereas India's Consulate in Guangzhou opens Southeast China for India. Connecting Arunachal Pradesh and Yunnan Province through Myanmar, China wants the old Stillwell Road, closed since the Second World War, reopened, whereas India is reluctant to have links through Arunachal Pradesh because of China's territorial claims.

A high priority was given to discussions on the sharing of river waters, even beyond the scope of the Brahmaputra (Yarlung Zangbo) and the Sutlej (Langqen Zangbo), forming a nodal forum of experts to discuss, according to the joint declaration, "interaction and cooperation on the provision of flood-season hydrological data, emergency management and other issues regarding trans-border rivers." India is very much concerned about Chinese plans of river diversions for its own needs because of the assumed consequences for India's Northeast.

Civilian Nuclear Cooperation

During his visit, President Hu seemed to carefully modify seeming Chinese opposition to the Indo-US nuclear deal of July 18, 2005. He suggested Beijing might now be ready to cooperate with India on civilian nuclear energy. This however, would be subject to China's international legal obligations. Hu Jintao had nothing to lose and everything to gain by adopting a positive approach to India on bilateral nuclear cooperation. If China would have continued to duck the issue, it would have only reinforced all the traditional political prejudices against it in India. The intended civilian nuclear cooperation between India and China marks a paradigm shift in bilateral relations.

15. Quoted in Sudarshan, V. (2006). "Hu Visit. Back to the Future". *The Outlook*, December 4. p.48

16. Historically Calcutta has been the centre of power of the erstwhile East India Company and till the shift to Delhi the capital of British Colonial India. It is the capital of West Bengal, where the Communist Party of India/Marxist holds since about 30 years the reins of power.

Nevertheless, we must hold our breath. For China's nuclear offer is conditional; that the proposed cooperation should be consistent with Beijing's international obligations. This caveat tells us that Beijing remains ambiguous on supporting the US led initiative to a change of international nuclear rules in favour of India alone. Although three other nuclear weapon powers, Russia, France and UK have supported the American initiative, Beijing has so far expressed a number of reservations on the nuclear deal. It has often suggested that change of rules should also apply to Pakistan, with whom China's relationship is as close as "lips and teeth". It has also suggested that any modification of the international regime cannot be just in favour of India. It is suggesting that if the US wants to do a favour for India, Beijing would like to oblige Pakistan.

New Delhi would have liked an explicit endorsement of the Indo-US nuclear deal and a promise to support it when it comes up for approval at the 45-nation Nuclear Suppliers Group. From the Chinese perspective as well, such an approach would have dramatically elevated the political significance of Hu's visit. Yet, India is not impatient and is prepared to wait. Given the scale of policy reversal in Beijing and its diplomatic style of cautious incrementalism, New Delhi values the breakthrough in the nuclear diplomacy with China. While keeping its fingers crossed, New Delhi is confident enough to know that Chinese leaders are pragmatic by nature and would not want to stand in the way of the Indo-US deal which has begun to acquire an unstoppable momentum. This view has also been expressed by the newly appointed Indian Foreign Minister Pranab Mukherjee after Hu Jintao's visit in India's Parliament (Lok Sabha).

Irrespective of the visible cooperation there still exist areas of conflict which cannot be neglected:[17] 1. The strong Chinese military cooperation with Pakistan with weapon systems which are directed against India; 2. India's "One China policy" is not reciprocated by Beijing with a "One India policy" given its claims on the whole of Arunachal Pradesh and in particular with regard to Tawang (see Section 3); 3. Beijing recognises "Pakistan occupied Kashmir" (PoK), respectively from Islamabad's point of view "Azad Kashmir", as a part

17. Vijay, Tarun (2006). "Playing Chinese Checkers". *The Hindustan Times*. November 12. p.10

of Pakistan, whereas it considers the Indian part of Jammu & Kashmir as "disputed"; 4. Chinese control over large tracts of Indian territory; 5. Chinese ambiguity with regard to India's claims for a seat in the Security Council, although the joint declaration during Hu's visit states: "China attaches great importance to the status of India in international affairs. It understands and supports India's aspirations to play a greater role in the United Nations."[18]

In existential questions of foreign policy, Indian political parties share a broad consensus. Hu Jintao met a delegation of both Indian Communist parties and the Forward Bloc—known for their anti-American positions—and accorded the Indian Left an important part to play in the strengthening of relations between China and India. On the other hand L. K. Advani, leader of Opposition in India's Lower House and former Deputy Prime Minister of the Hindu-Nationalist Bharatiya Janata Party (BJP), urged the Chinese President to let the Dalai Lama visit Tibet. "The Tibetans have their aspirations and the Dalai Lama is considered not just their leader but one of the spiritual leaders of the world."[19]

"While Hu's visit may not have resulted in substantive gains, both the Indian and Chinese sides have given the right political push for the relationship to expand and to deepen, but lot more needs to be done. As Hu remarked, the relationship has to bring in mutual trust. While the strategic seismograph of the Sino-Indian ties has come a long way from being estranged neighbours to cooperative strategic friends, a lot more political capital will be required by both sides before it can actually transform into a truly strategic relationship."[20]

C.V. Ranganathan, a former ambassador to China and as book author on India-China relations, a very liberal and balanced analyst, stresses, that "although no ground-breaking announcement has been made, the good thing is that in recent years such joint statements have become programmes for action to keep up the high level of momentum in our relations in various fields. India and China have, at

18. "India, China Adopt 10-pronged Strategy", *The Hindustan Times*. November 22, 2006. p.14

19. Iyer, Shekhar (2006). "Let Dalai Lama visit Tibet, Advani tells Hu", *Hindustan Times*. November 23. p.8

20. Shukla, Saurabh (2006). "Hu Does Give a Damn", *The Outlook*. December 4. p.40.

the very least, reaffirmed their commitment to deepen and diversify relations."[21]

Manoj Joshi, a well-known foreign and strategic policy analyst, argues, that Hu Jintao's visit "gives a feel of the texture of New Delhi's global policies. ...The broader Indian strategy, as probably that of China, is to enhance relations with a cross-section of important countries—the US, the EU, Japan, Russia, the ASEAN, South Africa, Brazil etc."[22]

The Pakistan Factor, Jammu & Kashmir (J&K), Tibet, Arunachal Pradesh

After decades of a one-sided political tilt towards Pakistan, including the support for Kashmiri self-determination and the UN resolutions on J&K, the then Chinese President Jiang Zemin suggested in a speech to the Senate in Pakistan in 1996 that New Delhi and Islamabad should put aside their dispute and embark on a mutually beneficial cooperation. During the Kargil War between India and Pakistan in the summer of 1999 and the military mobilisation during 2001/02, China maintained—although Pakistan's major strategic partner and largely responsible for its nuclear and rocket arsenal, together with North Korea—a measure of political neutrality.

India took note of this new Chinese approach. Yet, as it began to publicly revive its position that the Northern Areas are part of J&K, India has a natural issue with economic projects as well as the modernisation and upgradation of the Sino-Pak transport corridor across a territory that New Delhi claims to be its own. Equally troublesome is the different political treatment that China gives to Indian Kashmir. Even as it expands its presence in Pakistan occupied Kashmir and the Northern Areas, China is not willing to acknowledge India's control over parts of J&K. Beijing has also been dragging its feet on Indian proposals for cooperation across the disputed areas of Ladakh in the eastern parts of Kashmir. Extra-sensitivity to Pakistan's positions on J&K was apparently part of China's reluctance to exchange the boundary maps in the Western sector, where the territorial controls of Beijing, New Delhi and Islamabad converge.

21. Quoted in "Asian Giants Growing up, and it Shows", *The Hindustan Times*, November 22, 2006. p.14

22. Joshi, Manoj (2006). "The Sum of all their Fears", *The Hindustan Times*. November 22. p.10

Although India might not go public with its concerns, New Delhi would like to see China take a consistent approach towards different parts of J&K.

At a time when the government of the United Progressive Alliance (UPA) is engaged in sensitive and "purposeful" talks on Kashmir with Pakistan, the role of China, which is in control of different parts of the original state of J&K, has inevitably acquired a new political significance. For China, too, New Delhi's attitude to Tibet has become important amidst the ongoing "unofficial" talks with the representatives of the Dalai Lama, the spiritual leader of the Tibetan people who took political refuge in India more than four decades ago. In recent years, New Delhi and Beijing have traded mutual concessions on the two important territorial issues that have hobbled bilateral relations for so long.

Meanwhile, China has its own gripe on India's approach to Tibet that was at the heart of Sino-Indian tensions since the late 1950s. Beijing was happy with the "evolution" in India's position when Prime Minister Atal Bihari Vajpayee visited Beijing in June 2003. Since then India has declared that "Tibet Autonomous Region is part of the territory of the People's Republic of China." Beijing reciprocated by accepting *de facto* India's sovereignty over Sikkim. New Delhi also reiterated that the Dalai Lama[23] is not involved in any "political" activities on the Indian soil; but Beijing smirked and pointed to the Tibetan "government in exile" in Dharamshala, which it wants to be dissolved.[24]

In the run-up to Hu Jintao's visit, Sun Yuxi, the Chinese Ambassador to India, stated categorically in an interview to CNN-IBN, "In our position, the whole of the state of Arunachal Pradesh is Chinese territory. And Tawang is only one of the places in it. We are claiming all of that. That is our position."[25] China always claimed—as

23. Tikku, Aioke (2006). "Hu's Aafraid of a Simple Monk", *The Hindustan Times*. November 25. p.14

24. Excerpt from the joint statement: "The Indian side reiterates that it has recognized the Tibet Autonomous Region as part of the territory of the People's Republic of China, and that it does not allow Tibetans to engage in anti-China political activities in India. The Chinese side expresses its appreciation for the Indian position." Quoted in Chellaney, Brahma (2006). "Mastering Martial Arts", *The Hindustan Times*. November 27. p.10

25. "Close to Hu's visit, China claims Arunachal", *The Hindustan Times*. November 14, 2006. p.1

a part of its own territory and calling it "South Tibet"—Arunachal Pradesh,[26] a paradise for ethnologists and anthropologists, given its rich ethnic diversity.[27] Chinese insistence that Tawang always belonged to Tibet and that it cannot ignore Tibetan sentiment in a boundary settlement with India has complicated the border talks between the two nations. India of course insists that it will not cede Tawang under any circumstances. Given the fact that Sino-Indian border talks are about Tibetan territory, the "Dalai Lama actually occupies an unstated but crucial position" in any eventual boundary agreement.[28]

Given the complex nature of Kashmir and Tibet, New Delhi and Beijing have no option but to finesse their positions. While neither side is expected to get complete satisfaction, both will try and prevent Tibet and Kashmir from becoming obstacles to further improvement in bilateral relations. The Indian side claims categorically that Arunachal Pradesh is part of the Indian Union and that in a final border arrangement no people should be transferred, according to Dr. Manmohan Singh.

Economic Relations and Perspectives

Since the mid 1990s, China's economic growth has not just accelerated, but has acquired a strategic dimension all over Asia, including the Sub-continent. From being a relatively minor player in the economic calculus of India and Pakistan, China is now all set to emerge as one of the most important commercial partners of New Delhi and Islamabad.

Hu Jintao's visit showcased India's own trade relations with China that have grown so dramatically in recent years, after a negligible 260 Million US $ in 1991 to nearly US $ 24 billions. India and China want to reach 40 billion US Dollars in 2010,[29] quite in contrast to a study of the Federation of Indian Chambers of Commerce and Industry

---

26. Noorani, A.G. (2006). "Perfidy Re-incarnate. The BJP's Ignorance of China's Old Claims on Arunachal Pradesh is Shameful", *The Hindustan Times*. December 5. p.10. The author gives a short historical brief about the Chinese claims.
27. Ibid.
28. Phuntsok, Tashi (2006). "Play the Tibet Card", *The Times of India*. November 30. p.32
29. Bagchi, Indirani (2006). "India to Press Hu for Quick Border Settlement", *The Times of India*. November 5. p.9

(FICCI),[30] which envisages that the bilateral trade between India and China will hit 30 billion US $ in 2009: "...while India's exports to China are largely restricted to primary and resource-based products, Chinese exports to India are fairly diversified and include manufactured items as well as low and medium technology products. India's exports to China are highly concentrated with top three items—ores, slag and ash, iron ore and plastics—accounting for 71 per cent of the total exports. On the other hand, India's imports from China present both resource-based and manufactured products including electrical machinery and equipment, nuclear reactors, mineral fuels and products, organic chemicals and silk."[31]

This increased trade potential poses chances and challenges. FICCI identified 14 items for Indian exports to China, amongst them are light commercial vehicles, basic drugs, chemicals and pharmaceuticals, electrical machinery and is envisaging perspectives in the field of construction industry. Besides the potential for joint ventures and business collaborations, "major Chinese companies have set up offices in India in sectors such as machinery, metallurgical equipment, chemicals, automobiles, silk and engineering,"[32] considering the huge potential of India's domestic market.

Interestingly, the vast majority of the 150 executives in Hu Jintao's entourage belonged to small- and medium-sized industries. The representatives of major companies are already established in India, ranging from banks to heavy machinery, telecommunications and electrical appliances. "It is evident that the Chinese government plans to push its construction companies to tap India's infrastructure market in a big way."[33] As to demonstrate the strategic business approach with regard to India—also with a view to bolster the development of China's own backward regions—the majority of these industries are based in Southern, South West and Western China. At the eve of Hu Jintao's

30. Analysts in Delhi suggest this is a conservative goal, which might be reached well before the end of the decade. They suggest that US $ 50 billion could have been a more appropriate target.

31. Besides the Confederation of Indian Industries (CII), FICCI is the older one of the two leading Indian Employers Federations.

32. Choudhury, Gaurav (2006). "India China Trade set to hit $ 30 bn", *The Hindustan Times*. November 13. p. 20

33. Ibid.

visit, Wang Jinzhen, secretary-general of the China Council for the Promotion of International Trade, stated: "The process for applying for a permit to run a business in India is not transparent", also insinuating unfair treatment of Chinese firms in tenders in India.[34] Besides this habitual public Chinese criticism, already visible during earlier high-ranking visits from China, because—from their point of view—of a negative state of affairs, Wang Jinzhen stressed the overall positive direction of the relationship in the business field: "They should promote bilateral trade and put more emphasis on their complementary economics rather than competition. They should work together to expand their share of trade in the international market, rather than haggling over every dollar. In my opinion, Sino-Indian economic and technological cooperation is very promising and the two countries are moving towards economic, trade and sci-tech exchange."[35]

During the visit several agreements have been signed, in order to facilitate trade and mutual investments. Interestingly, Reliance Industries, India's largest private industry conglomerate[36], which is entering vigorously the booming retail-market sector with supermarket chains in India is sourcing many products from China. There is also a good chance, that a Chinese car-maker will produce in a joint venture a competitive model to the forthcoming Tata people's car, which is supposed to cost less than 2000 €.

While Beijing is set to emerge as India's largest trading partner ahead of the European Union and the United States—"in the last few years China replaced the USA as India's major source of imports during 2004-05"[37]—in the next years, that trend line has been evident all across Asia for a long time. China has already replaced the US as Japan's largest trading partner, and became a powerful force shaping the economic, financial and commercial flows in East, South East and South Asia. The impact of this growth is not just about incredible

---

34. Dasgupta, Salbal (2006). "Big Guys Missing in Jintao Delegation", *The Times of India*. November 13. p.13

35. Dasgupta, Salbal (2006). "Tortoise can never beat the hare: Trade Official Pooh-Poohs Talk of India Overtaking China by 2020", *The Times of India*. November 17. p.14

36. Ibid.

37. Although split now between the two brothers Mukhesh and Anil Ambhani.

numbers on growing trade volumes between China and other Asian nations. It is also about the Chinese economy sucking in the vast periphery on its long borders.

While India—together with China, the two fastest growing economies in the world ("Chindia")—remains hesitant to embark on a Free Trade Agreement (FTA) with China,[38] Hu and the Indian Prime Minister Manmohan Singh instructed a joint task force of experts to come up with recommendations for a more liberal trading arrangement between the two countries by October 2007. Dr. Singh also assured Hu that there will be no discrimination against Chinese investments in India, on political and security grounds.

China and India have been definitely competitors in their insatiable appetite for oil and other energy resources around the globe. Very often, China outwitted the Indian efforts. As a result of this visit, they will try to coordinate their endeavours to achieve energy security for both nations.[39]

Hans-Eberhard Dingels,[40] a highly experienced German security analyst, views this potential for cooperation nearly philosophically in the wider geopolitical context: "In the long run, China has to accept that India is an emerging superpower with all legitimate rights. Asia is a large continent in which there is ample room for China, India and Russia. Beijing is well advised to bear in mind that the most successful Chinese emperors were those who concentrated on the cultural and the economic well-being of their people."

Increased Chinese Economic Presence in Pakistan and repercussions on India

While the Indian security establishment is poring over the many agreements between China and Pakistan, including new ones on

38. Babani, Anoop (2006). "Dancing with the Dragon", *Business India*. December 3. p.140
39. Aiyar, Swaminathan Anklesaria (2006). "Free Trade Area or Yuan Trap?". *The Times of India*. November 26. p.16. S.A. Aiyar argues: "China keeps the yuan underpriced by at least 15 per cent. in a bilateral FTA, China would, through exchange rate manipulation, be imposing a hidden tax of 15 per cent on imports from India, while giving a hidden subsidy of 15 per cent to its own exports to India.
40. Dasgupta, Saibal (2006). "India Joins Oil-Buyers Club, Signs Key MoU with China", *The Times of India*. December 18. p.14

defence cooperation[41] like a collaboration on an airborne early warning surveillance system, signed by Hu Jintao in Islamabad after his departure from India, the most consequential outcome is the bilateral Free Trade Agreement (FTA), China's first such in the Sub-continent.

After deepening the strategic partnership with Pakistan, Hu Jintao brought Beijing's economic juggernaut right up close to India's heartland. Special Economic Zones (SEZ's) near Lahore have been set up for Chinese businessmen.

Over the last few years, there had been much talk about Punjab-Panjab cooperation across the Indo-Pak dividing line. Prime Minister Manmohan Singh, during his visit to Amritsar earlier in 2006, put across a vision for greater cooperation between the two provinces and their joint outreach to Afghanistan and Central Asia.

Given the resistance to creative ideas in the Indian national security establishment and the enduring burden of Indo-Pak relations that trumps the prospects for economic integration between the two Punjabs, it's Hu's turn to proclaim "*Chini-Panjabi bhai bhai.*" The FTA is expected to boost Sino-Pak trade nearly four times to $15 billion in the next five years. The FTA, however, is only one part of Hu's ambitious plan for economic integration between Western China and Pakistan. The SEZ projects in West Punjab will establish a framework for rapid expansion of Chinese investments in Pakistan. An agreement to develop a joint investment company will see Beijing financing a broad range of infrastructure development in Pakistan. Chinese and Pakistani companies have struck during Hu Jintao's visit 13 joint-venture agreements worth $ 3 billion, in chemicals, construction, energy and tourism.

Together the economic decisions announced by Hu Jintao in Pakistan amount to a qualitative transformation of economic relations between China and Pakistan. For pessimists in New Delhi, the emerging Chinese economic clout in West Punjab—a commercial alliance with one of the Sub-continent's most dynamic communities, the Punjabis—would mean Beijing is outflanking India in its own

41. Hans-Eberhard Dingels has been the head of the International Department of the Social Democratic Party of Germany (SPD) between 1964-1995 and afterwards foreign policy advisor to the President of the Socialist International (SI).

natural hinterland. For optimists, though, the Chinese success in cracking open Pakistan's market might create new opportunities for the rest of the world, especially India, and give a boost to the ailing and more or less defunct "South Asian Association for Regional Cooperation."(SAARC). New Delhi, which for years has been so focused on Beijing's military and nuclear partnership with Islamabad and chafed at its tilt towards Pakistan on Kashmir, will have to reckon with the fact that Chinese money might soon rule the roost in its neighbourhood. That China has an FTA with Pakistan and has emerged as the largest trading partner of Bangladesh last year should remind New Delhi that its failure to expand economic cooperation with its important neighbours is proving to be a blessing in disguise for Beijing. As its tight-fisted Commerce Ministry refuses to lift the many trade barriers with the neighbours and its cloistered security establishment prevents normalisation of bilateral relations with Pakistan and Bangladesh, India has in effect given China a free economic pass in the region.

While the Indian security establishment pats itself on the back for preventing Chinese investments in its border areas, Beijing's economic presence all across India's frontiers—from Pakistan in the West, through Nepal in the North and Bangladesh in the East to Sri Lanka in the South—will soon be a powerful reality.

From its own perspective, Beijing has no reason to limit its economic activity in Pakistan to the local market. It would like to gain access to other markets in the region, including those of India, Iran and Afghanistan. As Chinese capital begins the long overdue regionalisation of Pakistan's economy, Islamabad should be able to overcome its current political inhibitions on trade with India. The challenge for India, then, lies in creating SEZ's in East Punjab that could feed into and gain from China's new economic presence across the border. Underlying Beijing's new economic status in the Sub-continent is not just the expansion of the Chinese economy but the historic decision of the Communist leadership in 1997 to develop the Western regions of China. The Go-West strategy has brought into view the natural economic complementarities between Western China and the Sub-continent which share long frontiers and shared cultures. Seeking to globalise West China and restore its traditional connectivities to the South Asian markets, Beijing is modernising its transport corridors through Pakistan to the Arabian sea, built a rail line into Tibet which can be eventually extended to India and Nepal, and plans to develop the Irrawaddy corridor in Burma which brings it into the Bay of Bengal.

Hu's decisions to expand the Karakoram Highway that links Xinjiang in West China and Pakistan and establish trans-border connectivity with India underline the emerging economic role of China south of the Great Himalayas.

Scenarios and Repercussions on the Western World

"Asia is changing, and China is a principal cause." With that simple, yet dramatic first sentence in his book,[42] David Shambaugh, one of the world's leading Sinologists, highlights one of the most consequential developments of our times, the rise of China. Although much of the world is conscious of the unfolding economic miracle in China, very few are aware of the already manifest geopolitical consequences for Asia. The unfolding story of Sino-Indian relations is not just about the two countries. They are now poised to transform the structure of international relations.

Hu Jintao's political purpose in coining the slogan of a "harmonious world" is to counter the perception that a rising China is a threat to the world. In that sense the theory on building a "harmonious world" is an adjunct to Beijing's proposition that China's rise, in contrast to the emergence of new great powers in the past, will not be destabilising but peaceful. China today is conscious of its power potential and its emerging capabilities to alter the regional and international system. It is responding to the incipient resistance to its rise and finding ways to pre-empt it. India is a long way from strategising about its own future in the global order and finding an ideological wrapper for it. Hu's theory on a "harmonious world" revolves around four broad themes—effective multi-lateralism among states, development of a collective security mechanism, prosperity for all through common development, and tolerance and dialogue among diverse civilisations. The ideas that permeate Hu's world view—

42. China is also pressuring Russia to let it equip Pakistani JF-17s with Russian engines.

democratisation of international relations and non-intervention in the internal affairs of nations—have also been part of Indian foreign policy articulation. There is a big difference though. For Indians, principles are an end in themselves, for the Chinese, theories are meant to achieve practical outcomes.

China's emergence as an engine of regional economic growth has also influenced the politics and diplomacy in various parts of Asia, including the Sub-continent, and created the potential for crafting a new security order in Asia. The systematic planning of Hu Jintao's visit demonstrates, that China seems to be ahead of India as far as a deliberate foreign policy strategy is concerned, which holds true also for the South Asian region. New Delhi's security establishment is utterly unprepared to conceptualise let alone deal with implications of China's rise.

Arun Shourie, a former cabinet minister of the BJP-led government and a prominent ideologue of Hindu nationalism, states: "Our silence on Tibet speaks for itself. Similarly, it is well known that six years ago Vietnam offered us access to the strategic Cam Ranh Bay. We declined —so as not to offend China. Even six years after establishing a Tri-Services Command structure in the Andaman and Nicobar Islands, we have not positioned any significant assets there—in part out of the apprehension that doing so would bring us into direct contest with the Chinese footprint in Myanmar and Bangladesh."[43]

Vikram Sood, a former Secretary of the Research and Analysis Wing (RAW)—India's external intelligence agency—is also skeptical *vis-à-vis* the true intentions of China: "The Chinese have always believed that neighbouring states must be respectful and obedient. This may not cover India but the game to restrict India to the Asian Sub-continent remains Chinese policy. The tactics are simple: keep borders with India tranquil but do not solve the dispute, trade with India but arm Pakistan and wean away Nepal, Bangladesh and Myanmar. As India retreated strategically from Tibet over the last 60 years, Han Chinese and missiles moved in—the former to change the demography and the latter as an exhibition of Chinese muscle and future intent."[44]

43. Shambaugh, David (ed.) (2005). *Power Shift: China and Asia's New Dynamics*. Berkeley, CA: University of California Press.

44. Aroun Shourie, quoted in the *Indian Express*. November 8, 2006.

Therefore, Hans-Eberhard Dingels favours bold Indian initiatives of confidence building but also a true preparedness below the nuclear shield: "After the agreements on the nuclear potentials of India both in the civilian and military fields with the US, New Delhi has not yet come up with a new and bold strategy for the wider geopolitical neighbourhood. Instead of seizing the opportunity of increasing its influence by providing substantial security through mutual systems of collective defense, India might feel "protected" by its nuclear deterrent capacities but this could be a fatal illusion. The fragile political and military situation prevailing in Kashmir is still the most dangerous threat to India. What the country needs are highly mobile forces with a kind of firepower enabling them to resist any conventional military aggression and also terrorist attacks, operating from Pakistan respectively from within Jammu & Kashmir or of Al-Quaida fighters and destroy them."

Yet David Shambaugh argues, "despite the significance of China's rise, it is tempting to conclude that the Asian regional system is becoming 'China-dominant,' but such a conclusion is premature. This is decidedly not the case. China shares the regional stage with the United States, Japan, ASEAN, and increasingly India as well."[45] As India wakes up to the rise of China, finding a balanced approach to the northern neighbour will be one of its toughest foreign policy challenges. India must continuously expand its cooperative engagement with China and constantly work at the same time for a stable Asian equilibrium.

In the past, the lack of a co-ordinated pan-Asian view by Europeans, not a few did also for long years absurdly equate India with Pakistan within South Asia, a quite often complacent and condescending attitude for instance *vis-à-vis* Indian politicians and strategists—particularly in the pre-1998 period, moral preaching from a "post-modern" world view, combined with an obvious lack of a genuine interest in the country's external and internal affairs, as demonstrated by not a few Germans in various positions over the decades, led to a situation, that for instance Germany as a single European nation state does not count anymore as a major factor in the perception of the

45. Sood, Vikram (2006). "Chewing over China". *The Hindustan Times*, November 13. p.10

Indian power elite.[46] In the words of a leading Indian defence analyst, categorically stated during the SPD/The Greens government: "The Germans don't know what they want."

This Indo-Chinese summit clearly demonstrated, that only the European Union as a whole with a—although not yet existing—recognisable profile and a common political voice would be perceived as an equal by a self-confident China and India in Asian and international affairs. Till now, the former colonial power Britain is widely irrelevant *vis-à-vis* the influence of the United States of America in India, although parading in essential questions more or less as the spokesman of the various European countries. Only Europe as a political and diplomatic unit can interact adequately with these two emerging Asian giants, which are both firm believers in power politics and the 19th century concept of a balance of power. Yet, Europe—which has historically practised these concepts—could also, besides its marked economic presence, function as an influential catalytic force with its intellectual "software" of the history of the EU integration, the experiences of Commission for Security and Cooperation in Europe (CSCE) and Organization for Security and Cooperation in Europe (OSCE) or at a sub-regional level with models as practiced in South Tyrol between Italy and Austria.

A holistic political pan-Asian European view, with all its regional differentiations—particularly also with regard to South Asia—is inevitable, irrespective of particularistic national economic interests. Democratic India as the still weaker and more moderate force in Asia, compared to China, deserves in the current historical phase in Asian and international politics a decisively pro-active and empathetic European approach, particularly with a view to India's growing international status, but simultaneously restricted regional influence in South Asia, where China can be expected as an even more influential player in the years to come.

Important Indian opinion leaders perceive "old Europe" and also its various nation states as increasingly irrelevant for their country's future and its involvement in the modern world, an image which can

46. Shambaugh *op. cit.*: 23

be very much disputed and also with good reasons be falsified. The erstwhile obnoxious fixation on China, also by quite a few political foundations in Germany, should lead to a far more balanced dealing with these two big powers in Asia through coordinated European interactions. The German Presidency in the first half of 2007 should be therefore seen as a challenge and an opportunity for Europe and India, leading to innovative and broad-based interactions beyond the traditionally limited inter-governmental channels of communication.

On the other side it is perhaps possible, that through the economically expansionist "Imperial China",[47] as argued above, both the Indian and also the Pakistani political elites could regain or even transcend in the years and decades to come the forlorn worldview of the erstwhile Moghul dynasty (1527-1857) at its heyday, which included more or less the whole of South Asia and reached partly beyond to Central and West Asia. This would constitute a welcome new quality under the conditions of globalisation but also certainly a loss of influence by the Western and especially the European world in particular, measured not only by a reconstructive view over the last 200 to 250 years.[48] With war in Afghanistan, improved relations between India and Pakistan would not only benefit both of them, but it would also have in the wider context of this geopolitical region an indirect effect on the NATO forces there. "Neither country seems to have grasped the threat that the future holds out to both of them and the urgent need for them to face it together. Even less do they understand the opportunity that beckons if they succeed in doing so. We too are, therefore, on the edge of a spiral of violence that could stop our growth in its tracks and severely damage, if not destroy the Indian State. The only sure way to prevent it is to tackle its root cause—the continuing fallout within Indian society of the partition of India.

Herein lies the convergence of our interests. If we work together, India and Pakistan can help NATO to get out of the Afghan quagmire. And if we work together, we can eliminate not just the mechanisms

47. Buchsteiner, Jochen (2006). "Is Germany still relevant for India?" in Voll and Beierlein *op. cit.* pp. 241-243. This is also informally perceived in highest echelons of the German External Affairs Ministry.

48. Borrowed from Brahma Chellaney's article "Imperial China", *The Hindustan Times*. October 30, 2006. p.8

of terror in the Sub-continent but also the tissue of justification on which it feeds."[49]

Currently it seems, that the Chinese are really in the driver's seat with a targeted and holistic overview also in this part of the world, quite ahead compared to their main South Asian counterparts and in particular also India, with the result that there seems to be a nascent "Pax China" in the making. As a result India, with its own growing international stature, has recognised, that it requires, besides the Herculean task of internal social reforms at a large scale,[50] constructive co-players. Therefore, it is important to note, that Japan will extend to India "a special economic power status." "Multi-polarity at the global level cannot be squared with a China that seeks to keep Asia unipolar by either constraining or castigating India and Japan. Asia's bigger boats have to rise together if this is to be an Asian century of peace and prosperity. The alternative is bleak."[51]

The rise of China and India is already shifting the global balance of power from the West to the East and from Europe and North America to Asia: the world's centre of gravity is shifting from the Atlantic Ocean to the Pacific and Indian Oceans, as the Asian nations now seek the construction of an Asian economic community and a new security order. In retrospect, it was Jawaharlal Nehru, India's first Prime Minister, who proposed the idea of an "Eastern Federation" with India and China at the core. What then seemed to be a romantic idea is now being formally debated at the newly created East Asia Summit, where India and China are both members. For Singh and Hu, the challenge is to realise Nehru's vision on building a new Asia through Sino-Indian cooperation. The Western World and in particular Europe do still have a realistic chance, to play a prominent role in these processes, provided they play their strengths in a sophisticated and credible manner.

---

49. Compare the excellent and well-researched books of Dalrymple, William (2004). *White Mughals. Love and Betrayal in Eighteenth-Century India*. New Delhi, London New York etc.: Penguin Books and Dalrymple, William (2006). *The Last Mughal, The Fall of a Dynasty, Delhi, 1857*. Penguin Books, Viking.

50. Jha, Prem Shankar (2006). "The Stakes are High. India and Pakistan Need to Put Aside their Mutual Distrust". *The Hindustan Times*. December 04. p.10

51. Joshi, Manoj (2006). "Epic in Progress". *The Hindustan Times*. November 15. p.10. "A socially united country, where a Dalit or an Oraon tribal, too, has the same sense of the India they live in, as someone from the erstwhile dominant castes and the current elite, is a vital pre-condition for the evolution of a genuine Indian strategic culture."

Appendix

Time-Table of India-China Relations[52]

1949: India recognises the People's Republic of China, as the second non-Communist country to do so.

1954: India and China sign the "Panchsheel Agreement", Zhou Enlai visits India, Nehru Beijing, signing a Sino-India Trade Agreement.

1959: Zhou Enlai spells out China's claim to 40,000 square miles of Indian territory in Ladakh and the Northeast.

Escape of the Dalai Lama from Lhasa.

1960: Deadlock on the border issue during Zhou Enlai's Delhi visit.

1961: China occupies 12,000 square miles in India's Western sector.

1962: Indo-Chinese border war: China attacks from the Northeast to Ladakh, leading to a decisive Indian defeat and on the 21st of November to a unilateral ceasefire.

1963: Pakistan hands over 5,080 sq km of PoK (Pakistan Occupied Kashmir) in Aksai Chin to China.

1976: Diplomatic representation raised after a gap of 15 years to the ambassadorial level.

1988: Prime Minister Rajiv Gandhi's visit to Beijing is breaking the ice in the *de facto* "Cold War" between India and China.

1993: Prime Minister P. V. Narasimha Rao visits China: Signing of the "Border, Peace and Tranquility Agreement".

1996: President Jiang Zemin in India: Signing of an "Agreement on Confidence Building Measures" along the Line of Actual Control (LAC).

1998: Nuclear Tests—Pokhran II—by India (also Pakistan) and Krishna Menon Memorial Lecture by Defence Minister George Fernandes, where he declares "China as India's main enemy/adversary", followed by outrageous Chinese reactions. Beijing strongly condemns Pokhran II.

2000: President K.R. Narayanan visits China.

---

52. Bhaskar, C. Uday (2006). "Trade vs. Security". *The Times of India.* November 21. p.28

2001: Li Peng, Chairman of the Standing Committee of the People's Congress, visits India for 8 days and advocates a joint interest in a multipolar world order. Formation of an India-China Parliamentary Friendship Group.

2002: Chinese Premier Zhu Rongji in India, opening of a Shanghai-Beijing-New Delhi flight.

2003: Prime Minister Atal Bihari Vajpayee visits Beijing and acknowledges that the Tibetan Autonomous Region is an integral part of China.

2005: Visit of Prime Minister Wen Jiabao in India: "Sino-Indian Strategic and Cooperative Partnership" Agreement. Formulation of political parameters and of guiding principles for a solution of the border problems and "recognition" of Sikkim as a part of India.

2006: President Hu Jintao visits Delhi and Bombay. Ten point strategy and cooperation in civil nuclear energy.

4

The European Union and Regional Cooperation in South Asia

RAJENDRA K. JAIN

During the 1980s and 1990s, there has been a resurgence of regionalism in western Europe, North America, Latin America, and Asia. The resurgence of many of these regional groupings has been inspired by the example of the European Union in cementing political relations between historical rivals through increased trade, investment, and denser cultural and elite linkages. Economic regionalisation in the South has been accelerated as a result of the end of the Cold War, globalisation, and a keen desire to provide a stimulus to investment, employment, and growth in view of an increasingly competitive international economic environment. Efforts to establish a regional economic organisation in South Asia began in 1980 but it was only in 1985 that the South Asian Association for Regional Cooperation (SAARC) could be established—nearly three decades after the European Economic Community (EEC) was established in 1957.

This paper is divided into five sections. Section 1 makes a comparison of regionalism in Western Europe and South Asia. Section 2 makes a brief overview of EU-SAARC relations. Section 3 assesses whether the European Union is a model for South Asia. Section 4 identifies certain lessons of EU experiences in regional integration for South Asia. Section 5 discusses India's involvement in other Asian regional organisations. Section 6 makes some concluding observations.

Regionalism in South Asia and Europe: Similarities and Dissimilarities

The objectives and processes of regionalism in Western Europe and South Asia differ considerably including conceptually and structurally.

Historically and culturally, Western Europe exhibits several features of commonality which do not prevail in South Asia.

Firstly, SAARC and the European Union are very different. The European Union consists of "old" industrial, developed countries, which have graduated from the tasks of nation-state building. SAARC, on the other hand, still comprises developing countries with low incomes, which for decades has hampered the process of regional cooperation. Unlike South Asia, Western Europe is extremely cohesive and homogeneous in terms of ethnicity, language and culture. The common features of West European cultural conditions contributed positively to making international coordination feasible.

Secondly, EU member states are committed to parliamentary democracy, a multi-party system, free and regular elections, market economy and public institutions which are generally socially accountable. One of the major justifications for the admission of Greece, Spain and Portugal was to help stabilise, consolidate and strengthen democracy. Under the Copenhagen criteria, democracy has been established as a key criterion for membership of the European Union. On the contrary, the pattern of nation-building in South Asia has been complex and far from uniform. Apart from India and Sri Lanka, democratic experiments in other South Asian countries have floundered time and again. South Asia has several democracies (India, Sri Lanka, Maldives, Bangladesh, and Nepal, which has only very recently overthrown the monarchy), one monarchy (Bhutan), and a military dictatorship (Pakistan).

Thirdly, the motivations for regional integration in Western Europe and South Asia are different. Political motives behind European integration were the strong desire to avoid war and the political resolve to settle differences between two arch-enemies—France and Germany. European integration was also driven by the need to accelerate postwar economic recovery by the creation of a large common market, and expectations that an integrated Europe would lead to a new shared power in world politics and facilitate political independence in a world dominated by the super powers. Economic and military integration in Western Europe was considerably facilitated by an external federator (the United States). None of these internal or external factors were prime movers of regional cooperation in South Asia. The divergence in security perceptions of SAARC member states handicapped and dampened regional integration. South Asian regionalism was neither super power-sponsored, nor born to deal with an external threat. Such political-security concerns were entirely absent from the concerns of South Asian elites in the formation of SAARC, which arose from a purely economic rationale.

Fourthly, the perception of a common external threat was a significant factor leading to the establishment of both the European Economic Community amongst like-minded states. The United States as the external federator was determined to foster the economic and military integration of Western Europe so that it would not fall under communist influence. In the case of South Asia, however, there neither was an external catalyst nor a similar perception of an external threat. On the contrary, India was perceived as posing a threat to the security and territorial integrity of smaller states, against which security was necessary (which usually took the form of soliciting the involvement of external powers in subcontinental affairs) whereas India perceived her neighbours as being integral to its own security. The divergence in security perceptions of SAARC member states has impeded enhanced regional economic cooperation. The urge to form a regional economic grouping was internal, without the direct or indirect involvement of any external power.

Fifthly, market forces and powerful economic interests, both public and private, stressed the need for a large and secure European market not only as an outlet for their production and services, but also as a base to enable them to compete effectively in their international markets. The driving force behind the Single Market was more economic than political, more the urging of the business community than the initiative of the public. In South Asia, on the other hand, the process is from top-down, with a minimal role for South Asian business interests to become the driving force for fostering regional integration. All initiatives are government-sponsored and government-managed.

Sixthly, in the European Union, the process of regionalism remains an elite driven process. Each step towards coordination and cooperation in any one specific sector led to new awareness of obstacles, or of unexploited opportunities for coordination in related or other new sectors. This led to increasing international consultation on an ever-widening range of issues. Steps towards integration have not been dictated by economic logic.

Seventhly, Western Europe is characterised by the dispersal of strength in Europe. In the European Union, despite variations in size and population of member states, there is no one member which looms as large as India, or is the only unifying or dividing factor. The European Union has at least four, *viz.* the United Kingdom, France, Germany, and Italy, of a relatively similar population and more or less similar economic strength. No one power has the ability to dominate the region. South Asia, on the other hand, is characterised by the overwhelming predominance of India in terms of size, population, resources, potential of economic growth, military strength and a number of smaller states with no common border between them. While India borders or is adjacent to five SAARC member states, its neighbours have borders with none. This basic asymmetry colours the perceptions of India's neighbours, who have repeatedly sought to counterbalance Indian influence by seeking the involvement and support of external powers in the region.

A prime motivating factor behind the establishment of SAARC was the common fear of all small countries of domination by India and hopes that Indian ambitions to regional hegemony could be contained within the framework of a regional grouping. South Asian ruling elites have been more concerned about domination rather than working out a functional relationship with India. However, the problem of a large country in the region is not unique to South Asia. Non-European regions are characterised by the widespread "presence of one dominating regional power or the absence of a clearly and 'naturally' defined 'lead couple'."[1]

Eighthly, the European Union has supranational laws and institutions, comparable to those existing in national systems. Willingness of member states to voluntarily transfer competences to

1. Kuehnhardt, L. (2004). "The Global Proliferation of Regional Integration: European Experience and Worldwide Trends", *ZEI Discussion Paper* C136/2004. Bonn: Center for European Integration Studies. p.56.

supranational bodies organisations subsequently snowballed into other areas. This has not implied that nation states ceased to play a key role; the EU remains a "union of nation-states" and not a "United States of Europe". Member states have found different and creative ways of sharing sovereignty and pooling common interests and policies. This process is still evolving and it has given new content to policy-making in Brussels. In South Asia, however, there is a strong suspicion of supranational institutions modelled on the EU pattern. EU-style integration with the creation of similar institutional and legal structures and supranational bureaucracies was not preferred since it would erode national sovereignty.

Ninthly, what distinguishes South Asia from other successful examples of regional cooperation in the world is that, as a region, there is a lack of economic complementarity as exists in Western Europe. Thus, despite a common civilisational heritage, shared history, and potentially integrative eco-systems, member states of SAARC have still been unable to meaningfully and effectively cooperate in fostering greater economic development in trade, industry, and investment. South Asian economies are competitive rather than complementary and dependant to a large extent on the same product categories. Unlike the European Union where intra-regional trade accounts for over 65 per cent, intra-regional trade in South Asia is about 5 per cent of its global trade and intra-SAARC investment is only 1 per cent of its total investment. Trade continues to be constrained by several factors.[2]

Tenthly, unlike the principle of consensus or majority voting as is increasingly followed in the European Union, all formal decisions, including the choice of issues to be discussed and the areas in which to cooperate, must be unanimous.

Eleventhly, there is no formal institutionalised process for the

---

2. Four factors explain the limited intra-regional trade amongst South Asian countries: i) competitive export baskets, ii) high rate of tariff and non-tariff barriers, iii) lack of adequate transport and information links, and iv) political differences and a lack of willingness to create trade complimentarities. Dash, Kishore C. (1996). "The Political Economy of Regional Cooperation in South Asia," *Pacific Affairs* 69(2): 202 & 204, Summer. Also see Anam, M. and S.S. Rahman (1991). "Economic Integration in South Asia: An Explanatory Analyses in Trade, Investment and Finance", in Nanda K. Choudhury (ed.), *Canada and South Asian Development: Trade and Aid*. Leiden: E.J. Brill. pp.139-158.

discussion of bilateral political disputes among member states within the existing framework of SAARC. Political discussions have taken place, including on some bilateral issues, between the countries directly concerned, informally and on the sidelines of summits and Council meetings. Regular meetings of ministers did provide opportunities for informal "corridor talks."[3] These have contributed both to the diffusion of tension and facilitated resolution of some disputes. The exclusion of all contentious issues from the purview of SAARC is meant to keep the association "free from all superpower related uncomfortable questions." However, with changes in the post-Cold War era, it is doubtful whether this so-called "regionalism from below" would eventually prove viable.[4]

The differences in the evolution, geo-political milieu of the European Union and SAARC are significant in the identification of problems, of how policies are formulated, and what instruments are used for implementing those policies. There is therefore a natural difference in their priorities and institutional frameworks. Comparisons can therefore be misleading. The "experience of each region is different in terms of what factors bring them together, what problems they address and the advantages as well as disadvantages of a historic nature they may have".[5]

Thus, given the structural differences in the conditions and the institutional frameworks for the EU and SAARC one cannot apparently compare the incomparable since the former is perhaps the most successful experiment in human history and the most advanced and complex grouping and the latter is nearer the other end of the spectrum. SAARC is a little more than two decades old whereas the EU has reached where it has after five decades. The goal of SAARC is neither political nor economic integration; it seeks closer economic cooperation. Thus, the key word in SAARC is "regional cooperation"

---

3. European Union, Delegation in India. "EU/SAARC Relations". At *http://www.delind.cec.eu.int/eu/eu-saarc.htm*. 26 April 2002. p.2.
4. Ghosh, Partha S. (1991). "Domestic Political Constraints to South Asian Regionalism", in Dagmar Bernstorff and Dieter Braun (eds.), *Political Transition in South Asia: Regional Cooperation, Ethnic Conflict, Political Participation*. Stuttgart. pp.23-24.
5. Article by SAARC Secretary General Niharl Rodrigo (2003). in Yadu Nandan Bhandari (ed.), *11th SAARC Summit Special*. Kathmandu: Milan Weekly. Quoted in Nemsiri Mutukumar, "SAARC Summit Special: A Fantastic Fete". *Daily News* (Colombo). 15 July 2003.

whereas the key word of the EU is "integration".[6] The above discussion demonstrates the limits and possibilities of inter-regional comparative analysis.

The European Union and SAARC

Since the end of the 1970s, the European Community has been increasingly inclined to encourage and strengthen links with other regional economic groupings. However, from the outset member states of SAARC preferred to maintain their bilateral agreements with the European Community rather than develop a regional basis for future cooperation.

Initial contacts between the European Union and SAARC were initiated in 1988, but the first attempt to reach out to the European Community was made only in 1992. A Memorandum of Understanding (MOU) between the European Commission and the SAARC Secretariat (10 July 1996) envisaged cooperation in three main areas, *viz.* exchanges of information on issues of mutual interest, staff training to strengthen the functioning of SAARC institutions, and technical assistance. However, internal problems within SAARC have prevented "any effective implementation" of the MoU[7] even though agreement was reached to cooperate in certain areas.[8]

SAARC has had an informal Ministerial-level dialogue with the European Union on the sidelines of the United Nations General Assembly in 1998 and 1999. Indo-Pak tensions and the deployment of half a million Indian troops on the border led to heightened tensions in the region. After the withdrawal of troops in October 2002, the Dutch presidency sought to resume the dialogue in 2003 but it could not be held due to "logistical reasons". Thus, political dialogue

---

6. Rummel, Reinhardt (1995). "Transformation of the EC into EU: Its Salience and Relevance to Regional Peace and Development in South Asia", Paper presented at an international seminar on *SAARC 2000 and Beyond.* New Delhi. 22-24 March, p.11.

7. Memorandum of Understanding on Administrative Co-operation between the European Commission and the South Asian Association for Regional Cooperation. 10 July 1996.

8. These were: a) facilitating access to the Single European Market; b) implementation of the EU GSP scheme including cumulative rules of origin; c) drawing on the EU experience for the SAFTA process; and d) evolving common SAARC standards and harmonisation with international obligations, including certification, testing, etc. SAARC, Secretariat, *Regional Economic Cooperation: Inititiatives within the SAARC Region.* Kathmandu. November 2000. p.13.

between the EU and SAARC had, at best, been ad hoc. There was no mechanism to develop this along the lines of the EU-ASEAN dialogue.

Despite the keen desire of the European Union to enter into more concrete areas of activity (South Asian Free Trade Area [SAFTA], banking and development of norms and standards, WTO-related issues, transit and maritime issues and the area of environment, etc.).[9] SAARC's hopes that the EU-SAARC dialogue would become a regular feature and help identify new areas of economic and social cooperation as well as move to effectively implement projects and programmes in agreed areas of cooperation on which the two groups have some measure of understanding has not made much progress.

There has been very limited cooperation between the European Union and SAARC. Apart from the inclusion of SAARC in the Generalised System of Preferences Cumulative Clause of the Rules of Origin (w.e.f. 1 October 2000), there are really no meaningful EU-SAARC projects which are being financed by the European Commission. The lack of political cohesion among the SAARC members themselves, especially the uneasy relationship between India and Pakistan, makes the organisation "unsuitable as a political dialogue partner".[10] "Internal divisions" within SAARC which "have prevented much effective co-operation" with the European Union.[11]

SAARC found new dynamism with the adoption of the SAFTA framework treaty by the 12th SAARC summit (January 2004). This formally came into effect on 1 January 2006. Pakistan and India are scheduled to complete implementation by 2012, Sri Lanka by 2013, and the other four, *viz.* Bangladesh, Bhutan, the Maldives and Nepal by 2015. With SAFTA, SAARC had thus given itself "a clear economic

---

9. "SAARC Collective Efforts not Impeded by Inter-State Problems says Kadiragamar". *The Island* (Colombo). 1 October 1998.

10. Piening, Christopher (1997). *Global Europe: The European Commission in World Affairs*. Boulder. p.162. The Head of the European Commission's Delegation in Pakistan, Kurt Juul, also remarked: "The EU wanted to engage the SAARC in meaningful dialogue provided it had the will to put bilateral disputes on hold". *Dawn* Internet Edition. 1 November 2000. *http://www.dawn.com/2000/11/01top10.htm*

11. See European Commission. "The EU & SAARC: The Issue: SAARC's Low Level of Internal Co-operation". At *http://europa.eu.int/comm/external_relation*

integration agenda, which could provide the basis for closer cooperation with the EU."[12]

Graduating to a South Asian Economic Union

In January 2003, Foreign Minister Yashwant Sinha remarked that the EU was indeed an "example of regional cooperation that we in Asia could emulate." He urged that "we move forward from SAARC and think of a South Asian Union...[which] will not merely be an economic entity. It will acquire a political dimension in the same manner which the European Union has come to acquire a political and strategic dimension.... I am not suggesting an end to SAARC but an upgradation of SAARC into a South Asian Union."[13] At the Islamabad summit (January 2004), Prime Minister Vajpayee proposed a common currency for South Asia, but Pakistan considered this premature and this would have to await the solution of outstanding problems between India and Pakistan.

EU Becomes an Observer in SAARC

The Dacca summit (November 2005) endorsed the admission of Afghanistan as the eighth member of SAARC—the first enlargement since its establishment in 1985—and granted "observer status" to China and Japan. With India's support, the EU's application for Observer Status in SAARC was considered and approved by the 27th SAARC Council of Ministers meeting in Dhaka on 1-2 August 2006 apart from that of the United States and South Korea. All these five new observers, including the EU, would be able to attend the 14th SAARC summit being held in New Delhi from 3-4 April 2007. The meeting also adopted the "guidelines on observers" whereby observers would have to affirm that they agreed with the aims and objectives of the SAARC Charter and would be permitted to attend opening/closing sessions of the SAARC summit and meetings of the Council of Ministers. The

12. Commission of the European Communities, External Relations Directorate General, Directorate Asia (except Japan and Korea), Policy, Planning and Coordination. "Strategy Paper and Indicative Programme for Multi-Country Programmes in Asia, 2005-2006". p. 10.

13. Inaugural address by Sinha at the seminar on "South Asian Cooperation", organised by the South Asian Centre for Policy Studies, Dhaka. January, 10 2003. At *http://www.meaindia.nic.in/speeches/eam-10jan.htm*

observers would also be allowed to make statements at these meetings after advance circulation.[14] Other European states which have expressed an interest in becoming an observer of SAARC are Cyprus and France has also expressed a willingness to join as an observer state.

Is the EU a Model for SAARC?

Both the European Union and a number of scholars argue that the EU can "export" its norms and model of regional economic integration both horizontally and vertically to the global level, to global institutions (supranational governance) and that the EU can export its liberal vision of peace through democracy. "Sharing our experience of regional integration," External Affairs Commissioner Chris Patten pointed out, is perhaps "one of the most important international contributions that Europe can make."[15] The EU has "a natural interest" in regional integration, being itself a kind of project for regional stability and free trade.[16]

The notion of a EU is like "a more advanced model on a linear trajectory" has pervaded not only European discourse but often of those who seek to emulate it.[17] In the ultimate analysis, the EU is less a model to be emulated than "a laboratory" where "options for politics beyond the states are generated, for the taking."[18] It is a laboratory where "approaches to inter-state problems are tested, refined or rejected and where notions of justice beyond the state are progressively and tentatively operationalized."[19]

The prospects for the export of the EU model seem to be determined in important respects by the extent to which the European Union itself engages with other regions and provides them with incentives to integrate. This has most clearly been evident in the case

14. Remarks by Bangladesh Foreign Minister Morshed Khan, 2 August 2006, cited in Baruah, Amit (2006). "SAFTA meet to discuss Pakistan stand," *The Hindu*. August 03.

15. Remarks during his visit to India in 2001.

16. Patten, Chris (2004). "E.U. and India–Natural Partners", *The Hindu*. February 17.

17. Nicolaidis, K. and R. Howse (2003). "This is My 'EUtopia....': Narrative as Power," in J.H.H. Weiler, Iain Begg and John Peterson (eds.), *Integration in an Expanding European Union: Reassessing the Fundamentals*. Oxford: Blackwell Publishing. pp.342-343.

18. Ibid.: 345.

19. Ibid.: 357.

of the enlargement process in Central and Eastern Europe, the Mediterranean and the Balkans, where propitious conditions were present.[20]

In the extensive literature on South Asian regional cooperation, there are some who admire the achievements of European integration and wonder why some of its successes cannot be achieved in the subcontinent, especially in promoting regional trade and economic cooperation. Some argue that the EU is "structurally a more equitable arrangement and hence ethically as well as strategically more appropriate for South Asia, although obvious economic and political differences exist between South Asia and Europe."[21]

Many Pakistani leaders have hailed the achievements of the EU. The EU is an example of economic integration leading to political cooperation. It offered a model and other regional organisations can "learn immensely" from its experience.[22] Prime Minister Shaukat Aziz also remarked that the EU was the "best example of multilateral cooperation."[23]

Others maintain that the continuity of the EU and the failure of some regional experiments in developing countries, e.g. the Latin American Free Trade Association (LAFTA), the East African Common Market (EAC), etc. attest to the difficulty in drawing either "a parallel, or seeking a model for SAARC from the European case."[24] Thus, the "European integration process is absolutely exceptional and impossible to export as such elsewhere in the world."[25]

Since each region has developed its own approach towards regional

---

20. Peterson, John (2003). "The EU: Exportable Model or 'Jagged Little Pill'?: A Comment on Nicolaidis and Howse," in J.H.H. Weiler, Iain Begg and John Peterson *op. cit.* p.376.
21. Reed, A.M. (1997). "Regionalization in South Asia: Theory and Praxis", *Pacific Affairs*, Summer. p.250.
22. Remarks by Foreign Minister Khurshid Kasuri at a reception to mark EU enlargement, 1 May 2004. At *http://www.hipakistan.com/en/pdetail.php? newsId= en63700 & F_catID= 13 & f_type=source*
23. Remarks by Aziz to a delegation of EU ambassadors, Islamabad, 7 July 2005. "Shaukat asks EU for market access and technological help", *Daily Times*. 8 July 2005.
24. Khatri, Sridhar K. (1992). "A Decade of South Asian Regionalism: Retrospect and Prospect", *Contemporary South Asia* 1(1): 7.
25. Telo, Mario (2001). "Multilateralism and Regionalism in European Union and South Asia Relations," in B. Vivekanandan and D.K. Giri (eds.), *Contemporary Europe and South Asia*. New Delhi, 2001.

cooperation and it is based on its unique characteristics, although SAARC can learn from the EU and ASEAN experiences, it should pursue a strategy which is consistent with its geo-political milieu.

The European Union is not "a perfect model" for SAARC.[26] While an examination of five decades of European integration, which is often held up as "a goal or yardstick", may have some relevance in considering the future of SAARC. However, "the European experience was far from straightforward and was determined by circumstances unique to Europe. It is an experience, therefore, which is not easily transformed to other parts of the world."[27]

When asked whether the EU model wherein regional cooperation is a stepping stone to regional integration is a model, SAARC Secretary-General Nihal Rodrigo replied:

> The experience of the European Union where regional cooperation slowly built up to move comprehensive regional integration is attractive but cannot be duplicated exactly, given the particular South Asian context that we are looking at. Regional integration will be feasible for South Asia to the extent far-reaching, radical transformations in several sectors can be effected. The GEP [Group of Eminent Persons] identified many of these, such as transport, development of natural resources and energy, infrastructure development, joint ventures, industrial development, macro-economic policy coordination and so on.[28]

The European Commission has itself acknowledged that "there is no desire for European-style regional integration."[29]

Lessons of European Experiences for South Asia

South Asia is often compared to Western Europe in size and

26. Wagner, Christian (1994). "Regional Cooperation in Europe and South Asia: Can the European Union Serve as a Model for SAARC?", *Nepal Foundation Paper* 4. Kathmandu: Nepal Foundation for Advanced Studies. 26.
27. "Regional Cooperation and Integration in Europe and South Asia: A European Perspective," in Victor Gunewardena (ed.), *Regional Co-operation and Integration: Perspectives from Europe and South Asia.* Colombo: Delegation of the European Commission to South Asia. 1998. p.99.
28. Interview with Nihal Rodrigo, SAARC Secretary General, in "Attempts at Regional Cooperation in South Asia," *World Affairs* 3(1): 24. New Delhi, January-March 1999,
29. Communication from the Commission on "EU-India Enhanced Partnership," 26 June 1996, COM (96) 275 final, p. 8.

because of its diversity of languages, regions, nationalities, and cultural heterogeneity. However, there is hardly anything in common between South Asian and European historical experiences in the past three centuries.

The European Union fully realises the "difficulties that SAARC has in discussing political issues, and SAARC member states are not Europe." However, the Commission feels that the EC "can help consolidate the integration process through its economic influence in the region, its own experience in dealing with diversity, and its interest in crisis prevention."[30]

Amongst the lessons that the process of European integration can have for South Asia are the following:

1. *Conflict resolution and seeking compromises.* One of the lessons that SAARC can learn from the EC is that "states can be equal in association but be spurred by divergent interests to come together; that a union can comprise as its members countries motivated by diverse political goals; countries varying in size, economic potential and traditions and having to forfeit their national sovereignty to an extent but making decisions together for their common good can find common cause for integration."[31] By finding "common projects" that could produce common interests, overlap diverging interests and had little impact on core beliefs and values, it was possible in the European Union to transcend the values that had given rise to conflict in the first place.

   Just as the European Union has evolved different ways of sharing sovereignty, India can "be just as creative in devising ways of safeguarding the national interest while reducing the potential for conflict and increasing the mutual benefits of cooperation."[32] Many South Asian leaders have expressed a

---

30. European Commission, "The EU Relations with SAARC — Overview, The Issue: SAARC's Low Level of Internal Co-operation". At *http://europa.eu.int/comm/external_relations/saarc/intro*
31. Bastiampillai, Bertram in V. Kanesalingam (ed.) (1993). *European Community and South Asian Association for Regional Cooperation (EC and SAARC)*. Papers and Proceedings of the Workshop held in Colombo on 14 August 1992. Colombo: Friedrich Ebert Stiftung. p.47.
32. Hall, Andrew (2003). "EU as a Model for South Asia?", Paper presented at the *Information Seminar on the European Union for the Indian Media* organised the Delegation of the European Commission in India, at Fort Raichak, Kolkata. 5 May. pp.4-6.

desire to emulate Franco-German reconciliation. For instance, Benazir Bhutto asked: "Look at the European Community. France and Germany had age-old rivalries, but slowly they've come to terms with each other. Why can't we?"[33]

2. *Equitable distribution of benefits.* The process of European integration is replete with recurrent conflicts amongst member states over an equitable distribution of benefits and a constant quest to search for adequate solutions and compromises. To that end, the better-off states willingly accepted the redistribution of resources to less well-to-do states through instruments such as regional and structural funds in order to reduce disparities and to accelerate the process of economic development in poorer regions. Thus, the initial losses which weaker economies might incur through rapid trade liberalisation within the region, would need to be compensated through provision of compensatory financing on the lines adopted in the European Community during the integration of the Southern European countries into the Common Market.[34] In fact, there can be "no Europe without a commitment to solidarity between regions which means no Europe without a system which transfers resources to disadvantaged sectors and areas."[35] The unequal distribution of costs and benefits has been "the root cause" of all major conflicts experienced in integration systems among developing countries.[36] Some of the smaller member states of SAARC have been urging transfers somewhat similar to other trade blocs, to weaker economies to mitigate the adverse effects of more liberalised trade. India should be more magnimous in addressing these issues.

3. *Spillover effects.* Regional cooperation in Europe has fostered positive spillover effects: the gradual cascading of gradually

33. Cited in Weaver, Mary Anne (2003). *Pakistan: In the Shadow of Jihad and Afghanistan.* New York: Farrar, Straus and Groux. p.76.

34. See, for instance, "SAARC Chamber of Commerce and Industry Conference on *Towards SAARC Economic Union.* November 14, 1997. Proposal of the Group of Eminent Persons on Moving Towards a South Asian Economic Community" (n.p., n.d.), p.537

35. Guersent, Olivier (2001). "The Regional Policy of the European Union: A Balance and an Outlook," *Regional Studies* 35(2): 167.

36. Vargas-Hindalgo, Rafael (1979). "The Crisis of the Andean Pact: Lessons for Integration among Developing Countries," *Journal of Common Market Studies* 17(3): 213. March.

increasing economic cooperation will foster greater political cooperation. However, whereas "spill-overs can soften adversarial positions but they cannot dissolve them directly and quickly. Even if the favourable conditions of the European type can be realized, SAARC has to be supported by South Asian leaderships."[37]

4. *Implementing SAFTA*. The European Union would like to learn from the EU as a single market. The EU has actively supported the development of SAFTA by providing Euro 5 million for technical assistance.

5. *Procedural innovation*. SAARC can gain some insights and knowledge from EU experiences in institutionalised integration since there are certain common elements such as the guiding principles, flexibility and strength in practice, the handling of national and regional issues, the shape of different facets of integration, the role of particular institutions, and so forth. There is much that can obviously be learnt from the rich EU experience in fostering greater cultural cooperation amongst member states and enhancing the role of NGOs. However, replication of either the complex network of EU institutions or its ever-growing *acquis communitaire* is neither possible nor desirable.

   The European Commission maintains that the experiences of the European Union and its perspectives have "important lessons" for SAARC. In fact, "structural differences between both organisations are too great to simply copy institutions."[38] It is not desirable for SAARC to follow the costly institutional structure of the European Union. It would, however, be useful for its policy-makers to study which practices of the European Union can be adapted particularly in regard to formulation of proposals which are of common benefits to the region, principles on the basis of which the competence of regional bodies may be extended, and how economic integration and

37. Elsenhans, Hartmut (1997). "European Integration: Limited Automatisms and Implications for SAARC," *South Asian Survey* 4(2): 251.

38. European Commission, "The EU Relations with SAARC–Overview". At *http://europea.EU.int/comm/external_relations/saarc/intro*

political consultation could proceed side-by-side each reinforcing the other.[39] The European Union has always survived by finding innovative, creative solutions to problems. It has sought to do so by institutionalising consensus and compromises and the adoption of two new tools, *viz.* open method of cooperation (intergovernmental) and reinforced cooperation (Schengen, Euro).

6. *Managing asymmetry.* The "real utility" of SAARC, the European Commission opines, is that it helps member states to "manage their relations with their (much) larger neighbour India. Their ideal view is that of an organism that helps ensure respect of their sovereignty."[40] The Commission concludes that as an institution SAARC is not "an empty shell". It is not yet "a sound regional partner" for the European Union. It is, therefore, not realistic to think that SAARC could be modelled on the European Union, considering its internal conflicts and the specific geopolitical structure of South Asia, with an Indian core and dependent peripheral countries."[41]

7. *Role of civil society.* Europeans frequently stress the advantages of Track II diplomacy, which has been of considerable success in Europe. Cross-border connectivities and cross-community linkages have been of considerable importance because more contacts mean more interdependencies. For instance, the growing interaction between the two Punjabs, of India and Pakistan, have contributed to building a constituency for promoting Indo-Pakistan reconciliation. However, people-to-people contacts have their limitations. They are useful, but by themselves cannot trigger fundamental changes.

8. *A SAARC Parliament?* Drawing inspiration from the European Parliament, a suggestion was made in 1995 for the establishment of a SAARC Parliament, which could by its very nature "offer new types of political interaction which would be

39. Bhargava, Kant Kishore , Heinz Bongartz and Farooq Sobhan (1995). *Shaping South Asia's Future: Role of Regional Cooperation.* New Delhi. p.55.

40. See European Commission, "The EU & SAARC: The Issue: SAARC's Low Level of Internal Co-operation". *http://europa.eu.int/comm/external_relations/saarc/intro/template.htm*

41. European Commission. *SAARC: Geopolitical Exploratory Mission Report,* p. 21.

an important condition for increasing transactions, linkages and coalitions."[42] Drawing on the European experiences that help to harmonise the moral and political aspirations of different groups, the model of a SAARC Parliament would develop in two stages: In the first or transition stage, governmental influence would be high. In the second stage or final phase, popular participation will increase.[43] It seems that the creation of a SAARC parliamentary body is too visionary at present.

India and Asian Regionalism

Frustration with the inability of SAARC to make any meaningful progress in promoting regional economic cooperation led India to reach beyond South Asia towards East and Southeast Asia. India has participated in the establishment of new regional and sub-regional groupings like the Indian Ocean Rim Association for Regional Cooperation (IORARC), the Bangladesh, India, Myanmar, Sri Lanka and Thailand—Economic Cooperation (BIMST-EC), the Mekong-Ganga Cooperation Grouping, and was granted observer status in the Shanghai Cooperation Organisation (established in Sept. 2001) in July 2005.

In recent years, India has embarked on an aggressive strategy of concluding Preferential Trade Agreements and Free Trade Agreements (FTAs) with Asian and other countries. In recent years, India has been advocating the establishment of an Asian Economic Community, which would act as an anchor of stability, prosperity, and closer economic integration. India's espousal of the vision of an Asian Economic Community with ASEAN, South Korea, Japan, China and India as the "five pillars which may form the initial core to drive Asia's emergence as the center of gravity of the global economy." This idea is built on the fundamental realisation of the new dynamics in Asia and existing synergies.[44] Despite reluctance on the part of China,

---

42. Sondhi, M.L. and Shrikant Paranjpe (1995). "SAARC Parliament and the Pursuit of Stable Peace in South Asia," *Policy Studies* No. 2. New Delhi: Conflict Management Group, Centre for Science Policy, Jawaharlal Nehru University. p.11.

43. Ibid.: 41.

44. Inaugural address by Foreign Minister K. Natwar Singh on "Changing Security Dynamics in Eastern Asia" at the *Seventh Asian Security Conference* organised by the Institute for Defence Studies and Analyses, New Delhi. 27 January 2005. At *http://meaindia.nic.in/speech/2005/01/27ss01.htm*

many ASEAN countries have felt that India could bring its own synergies and dynamism to the grouping. They also realised the value of engaging India for greater political, security and economic balance in the region instead of it being dominated by China. If an Asian Economic Community eventually emerges, it would be useful in countering the agenda-setting capabilities of the United States and the European Union. It would contribute to trade liberalisation, strengthen inter-regional linkages, and promote access to extra-regional markets. It can also enable Asia to play a larger role in determining the rules that govern the international economy, which have so far been excessively dominated by the United States and the European Union.

As long as South Asian regionalism remains underdeveloped and does not make much headway in closer economic cooperation, there do not seem to be bright prospects of developing an inter-regional Europe-South Asian relationship. As European interest shifts to greater engagement with China and India, inter-regional relations with ASEAN or SAARC may become a less dynamic aspect of Euro-Asia relations.

Conclusion

From its very inception, SAARC was not based on any given model or paradigm. The experiences gained by a particular organisation are "unique" and may not necessarily be replicated in another regional organisation. No two regions can ever be similar in regard to the motivations, imperatives and strategies for regional cooperation in view of the differences in history, socio-economic and geopolitical conditions. There is hardly anything in common between the South Asian and European historical experiences of the past three centuries. However, the successes and failures of earlier organisations can be of relevance for organisations which were established much later since they may provide useful insights and perspectives to them in deciding their course of development.[45] There are obvious limitations of the applicability of the experiences of the EU for South Asia because of

45. Iftekharuzzaman *et al. (1989)*. *ASEAN Experiences of Regional and Inter-Regional Cooperation: Relevance for SAARC*. Dhaka: Bangladesh Institute of International and Strategic Studies. p.109.

the different geo-political and strategic environment prevalent in both regions. Moreover, as Kishore Mahbubani argues, there is "a flawed element in European strategy in the assumption that the rest of the world will follow the European social idea. This belief in the superiority of the Western idea creates a unique weakness or blindness for Europe."[46]

While SAARC could learn many things from the European Union, it is essential to "remember our own specificity and we have to develop our unique model" about regional cooperation.[47] The model that was being evolved for SAARC was in accordance with the realities of the region, not seeking to melt our bilateral relationships into a common regional integrity but rather to fit South Asian cooperation into our respective foreign policies as an additional dimension.[48]

The differences in the origins and evolution of SAARC and the European Union on the other signifies that regionalism acquires its own peculiar features in a region and that a region cannot possibly hope to either replicate or emulate a pattern of goals or events found elsewhere. While there are some lessons that can apparently be derived from the European Union, the conditions in South Asia are too different to permit a replication of either strategies or models of cooperation.

---

46. Mahbubani, Kishore (1995). "The Pacific Impulse", *Survival* 37(1): 110, Spring.
47. European Institute for South and South East Asian Studies, *The Outcome of the 1992 SAARC Summit and Prospects for a SAARC-EC Agreement* by H.E. Mr Kant Kishore Bhargava, Former Secretary-General of SAARC and Mr Ross Massod Husain, Chairman of Pakistan Futuristics Foundation and Institute, Monday, 1st June 1993 (Brussels, 1993), p.9.
48. Address by Pakistani President Zia-ul-Haq at the inaugural summit at Dhaka, December 1985. Cited in Khilnani, N.M. (1987). "India's Political and Economic Politicies towards Her Neighbours," *The Round Table* (London). No.301. p.54.

5

The European Union and the Indian Sub-Continent

A Marriage of Convenience

SURYA KUMAR BOSE

There have been innumerable articles, lectures and discussions on the topic of off-shoring as well as on the invasion of the Indian IT force onto European shores! I do not intend adding to the already overcrowded collection of material on the subject. Nor do I intend throwing a load of statistics and charts at the reader. Having spent over quarter of a century in Europe, mainly in Germany and Austria, and having played a not too unimportant role in trying to bring the Indian sub-continent closer to Europe, both in mind and matter, I would like to share some of my thoughts and experiences, which may be of some help to future Euro-Indian ventures. I shall use Germany as an example and would then try to bring in the neighbouring countries of the European Union into the arena. I shall also restrict myself to the subject of Information Technology and its enabled services.

Before we talk about Euro-Indian relations, let us first tackle some of the basic assumptions and presumptions that exist in the minds of many. It would be very presumptuous to try and transplant the Indo-American experience to the Euro-Indian platform. The relationship between India and the USA in the academic as well as in the IT and IT enabled services is a totally different ball game; it was built up in a different manner—mostly through those Indians who went to the US for higher studies, and after having established themselves there, sought business links with India mainly through their alumni and sometimes through family connections. USA being what it is—a country with unlimited opportunities—was a breeding ground for entrepreneurship, which cannot be said of Germany or other European countries where protectionism has played a major role till recent times. The India-UK relationship is another story altogether; the interaction having started from the colonial period—and as such it is not surprising to find the Indian community in the UK as an integral part of the society. The business world there is dominated by Asians and their presence is felt in almost every sphere of activity. As a result the statistics on off-shoring as far as the UK and India are concerned could be quite misleading.

I shall henceforth concentrate on Germany and then take it on to the rest of Europe. Germany is known for its adherence to perfection and this sometimes may become a hindrance to modernisation of its IT systems. The age-old proverb "never change a running system" is one of the favourite mottos of IT chiefs in Germany, be it in large multi-nationals or in SME setups. Germany has been a pioneer in the area of science and technology but strange as it seems, in the area of Information Technology, a lack of faith in something new and the absence of a spirit of adventure in deploying modern methods and technologies have been responsible for the rather antiquated state of IT systems in German companies. The longer one waits, the more difficult it becomes to overcome the huge back-log and modernise the system. This is a tricky situation and is a continuous source of headache for the IT vendors in the country. Most companies have cut down expenses for the training of their own staff and as a result the level of knowledge is not always up to date. In spite of all this, there is enough expertise available in the country although a very small part of it is put to use and the remaining majority of IT professionals are either frustrated or let themselves be used for mundane jobs in the maintenance of old and antiquated systems. As a result a rather false impression of German IT professionals is exposed to the outside world—and the so-called Global players from India feel that they can teach them a thing or two! This has led to quite a lot of misunderstanding, which could easily have been avoided. Experience is more valuable than sheer theoretical knowledge and that's where German software professionals have an edge over their Indian counterparts. A combination of the two would produce excellent results and we should strive to bring about such collaborations.

It is a fact that India produces thousands of IT professionals every year, but without sufficient exposure to the real world of Information Technology, all these young professionals are just raw material, which have to be polished and prepared to become finished products. I have always been of the opinion that universities and technical institutes should work closely with the industry, so that students can do real life projects under so-called research and development schemes, while they are still studying. This would help shorten the incubation period of these budding professionals. This is a procedure followed by most institutions in Germany and elsewhere in Europe. Also, it is necessary to build up a strong local base in India for the professionals to get their hands-on training. In the mid 1980s when there was very little implementation of IT in India, the export market definitely played a major role to generate revenue and simply just for survival.

Even though the entire Indian IT services industry represents only a fraction of IBM Global Services, it is having a dramatic impact on the global consulting services industry. Giants in the industry like IBM, EDS, Accenture, Cap Gemini and others are expanding rapidly in India to benefit from the low-cost, high-quality workforce, while Indian software firms are expanding in the US to create the closer customer relationships required to compete in providing high-end consulting services. This is not happening to that extent in Europe and particularly not in Germany. As far as the US is concerned, this cross-movement of jobs and labour will create an interesting competitive dynamic as the cost structure converges and firms compete to provide knowledge leadership—concept, technology breakthroughs and process innovation. Unless similar trends can develop in Germany and elsewhere in Europe, similar dynamics will not evolve and Europe will be the loser.

To become recognised global brands and move up the value chain, Indian software firms must promote knowledge leadership, create incentives to innovate, and foster efforts to enhance cultural alignment. Unfortunately till date, most Indian IT companies, including our global players, have pioneered new development for companies like IBM, Microsoft, Hewlett-Packard and others without getting a branding for themselves! They have to build up their own brands to become competitive in the global arena as software vendors and not just service companies.

The Indian IT services industry continues to make inroads into the global marketplace with its global delivery model (GDM), which uses a mix of onshore and offshore development. "Offshore outsourcing is at the core of the Global delivery Model[1] which refers to the philosophy of: (a) breaking pieces of work into logical components, and (b) distributing these components geo-locationally, to perform them where it creates the maximum value." The concept is sound and does make a lot of sense. Unfortunately, the socio-political environment in Germany and most of the European Union countries, are not ideal for such an implementation without making certain adjustments on either side. In 2005, the big three Indian IT service firms—Infosys, Tata Consultancy Services and Wipro—surpassed $2 billion in revenue and reported an astounding compound annual growth rate of more than 30 per cent, most of it in the USA. Due to dramatic cost advantages overseas, the GDM puts significant economic pressure on US firms to adopt competitive offshore-onshore development strategy. Major IT service companies like IBM Global Services, Accenture, Ernst & Young, Cap Gemini, Deloitte, EDS and others are aggressively expanding in India to benefit from the GDM. The same cannot be said of European IT service companies, which operate only in the European sphere. But there is a definite trend in that direction and companies here have to take it seriously if they want to stay competitive.

Cultural alignment and closer customer relationships are key to competing successfully in providing high-end consulting services. Further, the perennial uncertainty of obtaining visas is a big hindrance to any kind of planning. Also the high unemployment rate in the IT field is not congenial towards off-shoring or onsite deployment of personnel from Indian companies. The apparent arrogance of some of the "Indian Global Players" does not help in establishing rapport with the local IT community. Keeping all this in mind, I personally feel that there has to be a healthy mixture of onsite and offshore participation, the onsite part comprising mainly of local professionals, if we want to create a win-win situation and an amicable work atmosphere. Although, a certain amount of interchange should take place to foster

1. Infosys Global Delivery Model.

mutual understanding. Language is another issue that cannot be ignored. Europe certainly provides a diverse choice of languages and we have to take that into consideration when doing business in the European Union. In the sphere of Information Technology, English has become the *de facto* standard of communication but when it comes to "User Interface" the national language of the country plays a major role. Although, English is accepted as one of the Indian languages and most students passing out of Indian colleges and Universities speak and understand English reasonably well—still some of the accents are at times very difficult for a foreigner to comprehend! So, a little patience on either side would work wonders.

Now let us take a look at the options that Europe and India have in trying to create a global balance in the area of off-shoring. Germany or France or any of the other countries of the European Union for that matter—are on their own too small an entity to offer India a "Partnership status" comparable to that of the USA. Europe has to balance out the heavyweight that the USA provides as an off-shoring customer—to make it feasible for Indian companies to concentrate their efforts in the European Union and also to send their best people there. Germany being the most powerful economy in the European Union, plays a key role in setting the parameters for off-shoring. Off-shoring could create new wealth for Germany, but only if it adopts the structural reforms needed to reemploy its displaced workers. A recent survey shows that about 40 per cent of Western Europe's 500 largest companies have already begun moving their service operations abroad. This trend, made possible by the digital revolution and the dramatic fall in international telecommunications costs, is fuelling protectionist sentiment while creating waves of anxiety among white-collar workers once protected from global competition. This of course is a very natural reaction. One should remember that the backbone of the German economy is its "Mittelstand" (the SME sector) and not the large companies. Hence, we should be sensitive to the requirements of the Mittelstand. As opposed to large multinationals, the Mittelstand has not been exposed heavily to off-shoring and hence are quite hesitant in such matters. Transforming business processes as part of a strategy to offshore back-office functions can release massive new revenue opportunities, even more valuable than the obvious labour cost savings that come with off-shoring. The bandwidth available in the telecommunication links within India is still quite low. There has to be a marked improvement in this sector if Indian companies would also like to provide remote support and monitoring of systems, which is another very promising area for off-shoring or outsourcing. There also has to be better understanding amongst the innumerable telecom providers across the country. The local loops at times are bigger bottle-necks than the entry into the country from outside!

To get the full value of off-shoring, Germany needs to create jobs in high-value-added occupations, not just at the lower end of the wage scale. To do so, it must address the inappropriate product market regulations that stifle competition and innovation. Without pressure from competitors, companies have little incentive to innovate and boost productivity on an ongoing basis. Although some people might think that higher productivity means fewer jobs, the empirical evidence shows that it actually generates economic growth in mature, advanced economies such as Germany and the United States. Higher productivity lets the companies that achieve it offer consumers lower prices and better value, thus stimulating demand and allowing more productive competitors to take market share from less productive ones. This is where fine-tuning of onsite and offshore is of utmost importance. One of the worrying factors in Germany and in other parts of the EU is the shrinking workforce because of an aging population. India on the other hand has a very young workforce and in great abundance. The logical conclusion would be to supplement the shrinking workforce in countries like Germany by providing the necessary workforce from India. But this is easier said than done. The complex socio-political problems that would then crop up, would be difficult to solve. We have to learn to co-exist and develop a healthy respect for each others' capabilities. Traditionally outsourced IT services, such as hardware and software maintenance—which have seen very little off-shoring to date—will probably drive the next wave of growth. Off-shoring should increase more rapidly in business processes than in IT services; banking and insurance will likely lead the way.

Further growth will come from new "offshore-only" services that go beyond the simple replication of onshore ones. But all this would require a very well organised infrastructure in India. Infrastructure is an area which has been grossly neglected and needs to be tackled at all levels and with the utmost priority. Without a sound infrastructure in the field of telecommunications, transport, road systems, power-supply and a host of others, IT or IT enabled services will not be able to grow or even maintain its present status. The EU can contribute in a big way through joint-venture projects in all aspects of infrastructure. This would also go a long way in bringing the EU and India closer. This "marriage of convenience" would then culminate in a "marriage of purpose."

6

European Union and India

A Longue Duree Approach to the Evolving Relationship between Two Civilian Powers

MARIO TELO

A Peace by Pieces Perspective: EU India 'Strategic Partnership' and its Theoretical Implications

The landing of Vasco de Gama in Cochin in 1498, a potential meeting between two cultures, became the starting point of several tragedies, largely provoked by several European national imperialisms, Portuguese, Dutch and British. However, there is a discontinuity in the European history of the 20th century. The risk the world is currently facing is not at all the one of the European Union's empire.[1] Rather, the post-Cold War world order is oscillating between US-unipolarism on the one hand (and unilateral policies of the sole remaining superpower) and anarchy on the other hand (terrorism, diffusion of WMD, failing states). Both Europe and India are facing an open option: they could be either victim of such an evolution or driving actors of a "new multilateralism", where interregional and bilateral dialogue and cooperation, human rights protection, accountability and transparency towards public opinion may constitute new innovative features of a more just and stable global governance.

Are India and Europe making concrete steps in this direction despite global and regional instability? According to my modest experience, a major Indo-European conference in 1998 celebrating in Cochin and Calicut the 5th century of the De Gama landing, concluded

1. The concept of Empire is analysed in this paper as a tool for understanding the external relations. There is no room to discuss any other concept of empire, related to the internal EU institutional polity, as a medieval empire, according to the Dante understanding (De Monarchia) revived by "new-medievalists" as Fritz W. Scharpf, Susan Strange and others.

by emphasising the need of a new era of constructive dialogue, beyond the limits of a mere economic and trade partnership. Seven years later, some has been done. A "Strategic partnership" has been established between India and the EU. What does that mean in concrete terms?

The relationship between the EU and India is a crucial piece of global governance, where two major world democracies may show themselves capable of providing an input to reforming global governance. However, we are aware that this relationship is part of a triangle where the US represents the third, active and relevant corner, as shown by the triumphal visit of G.W. Bush to India in March 2006, (supporting the Indian nuclear programme). In this challenging context, strengthening the EU-India bilateral partnership may make global governance less asymmetrical and the relative weight of the sole superpower less fundamental, than in the past. The EU-India "Strategic partnership" established in 2004 has been the positive result of a long process[2] and currently entails a multidimensional framework for enhanced cooperation. In September 2005 an action plan was able of setting concrete measures.

What does the "Strategic partnership" and the "Action plan" concretely mean? The Action plan signed in New Delhi by Tony Blair (as rotating President of the EU council) and Indian Prime Minister, M. Singh, on September 7th 2005, is already partially implemented, according to the monitoring summit of Helsinki (Oct. 2006). It includes four chapters:

1) A political chapter, enhancing the political cooperation, including in the framework of the UN and allowing a dialogue on the very notion of pluralism, social diversity, human rights, effective multilateralism, and strengthening the UN role. Cooperation in training forces for peace keeping missions and post-conflict reconstruction tasks. The common fight against terrorism is situated in a global and regional security dialogue perspective, including disarmament and non proliferation. The

2. A positive step has been accomplished at the Lisbon bilateral meeting in Spring 2000 during the Portuguese EU presidency , prepared by the Commission expertise (see EU Commission communication of 1996 on India). However, on the one hand, the decision of India and Pakistan to build up a nuclear military capacity, the coup d'Etat in Pakistan, the anti-Pakistan evolution of SAARC, and, on the other hand, the European Agricultural Policy and its protectionist effects on trade, have been the major obstacles.

large array of common antiterrorist policies places at the top, mutual information, coordination of intelligence agencies, fight against the financial basis, and other civilian measures within a multilateral framework. Furthermore, the EU is becoming an observer in SAARC (New Delhi, April 2007) and India is becoming a member of ASEM (Asia-Europe Meeting).

2) Trade bilateral partnership is becoming central, aiming at promoting trade and investments. Not only a mixed high level group has formulated clear recommendations, emphasised by the 7th summit in Helsinki 2006, but the serious uncertainty of the Doha Round in 2006 is providing this chapter with a major political role: will a bilateral free trade area overcome past mistrust and the current limits of bilateral trade cooperation?[3] The EU is traditionally perceived as a trade fortress by Indian public opinion, not only regarding the agrarian sector, which constitutes a major bilateral problem (see the controversial "EU-India Business summit" and the critical declarations of the Indian part, among others by the Minister, Kamal Nath in 2005). From the EU side, free trade and capital investment negotiations should be accompanied by dialogue on human rights, labour rules,[4] and environmental standards.

3) As part of the economic policy chapter, the EU will take part as an advisor of Indian economic reform, strengthening cooperation in space research and direct Indian participation in the satellite recognition project "Galileo" (which is the most advanced project as knowledge and ICTs are concerned, including a very broad spillover effect as far as technological cooperation is concerned). New joint working groups have already been set up regarding science and technology:

3. In 2005, EU exports of goods and services accounted for 25 Bn Euros (only 2% of EU exports). Foreign Direct Investments from the EU to India accounted for 1Bn (1.4% of the total of EU direct investments and focus on telecommunications, energy and transports. However, already with this limited number the EU accounts for one fourth of total FDI, higher than from the USA and Japan put together (see Sachdeva (2006). *Rising India. Working with Europe to Shape Globalization*. Transcultura Network Conference, Brussels. November).

4. In this framework, European trade unions are supporting the campaign "Stop child labour. School is the best place to work", which fosters on the one hand a constructive dialogue with Indian parliament (ratification of ILO convention) and on the other hand, a financial support by the EU.

biotechnologies, genomics, nanotechnologies, transports, energy policy (including alternative energies and all what matters for energy security), food, climate change, sustainable development, and agrarian policy.

4) A cultural cooperation programme, based on the famous "EU-India cultural declaration" of 2004. The first point is the people-to-people understanding. Inter-parliamentary and civil society dialogue is fostered. In this framework, Indian migration flows should be seen as an extraordinary opportunity for EU countries, making cultural dialogue a broader issue (as argued by the mixed High level group settled by the EU-India summit of 2000 wishing among others an easier visa policy). The second concrete issue: are student exchange programmes in the framework of "Erasmus mundus". Third, networking EU and Indian universities, for example by opening the 6th and 7th research framework programme of the EU commission and adapting existing bilateral relations within the new ERA Net initiative.

The Action plan constitutes a framework and, more, a road map for fostering bilateral cooperation. It may be the starting point of a dramatic change in the EU-India relationship. Of course, skepticism is justified by previous disappointments. However, once a year an India-EU summit is monitoring the progress of the action plan implementation and the first partial monitoring which took place in Helsinki was positive about implementation, while a general assessment is expected in 2008. Very much will depend upon the external variables of the evolving world disorder.

European Union and India: A Longue Duree Approach between two Civilian Powers?

In the early 21st century globalisation looks fragile and nobody any longer believes in the optimistic myths of the post 1989 years: "the end of history" and a "win-win global market". The successful Indian novel by Kiran Desai is a symptom of such a broadly spread out disappointment, scepticism on the Western model, or, even better, of such a "*désenchentement.*"[5] Globalisation looks as conflictual and many countries and people feel as outsiders. However, what we are still lacking is a shared concept of understanding the current evolution of the partially globalised world. The heterogeneity of the global system is proved by the conflicting coexistence between unipolar, multipolar, anarchical and multilateral tendencies. Unipolarism dominated the debate between 2001 and 2005. In our understanding, neither the concept of the Western Empire nor the concept of classical military power are useful in understanding the current international roles of the EU role within the Western world. In Europe there are several historical and theoretical references for alternative notions and practices of international power based on peaceful action and influence, while measurable in term of efficiency.

The precondition for an appropriate conceptualisation is to make us free from misleading concepts, belonging to the past. This paragraph will focus on the obsolescence of the unipolar concept of 'empire' and on the contradictions within the devised western world. Let's start by underlining that it is interwoven and often confused with that of 'imperialism'. The latter is in no way applicable to the EU as it is intimately associated with the economic aspect of inter-imperial conflicts, of the end of the nineteenth and beginning of the twentieth centuries, i.e. a particular stage of the classic multipolar world which saw the colonial expansion of a limited number of European powers, namely the UK and France, and competition for access to new markets. John Hobson's economic analysis of imperialism as a solution to the domestic imbalance between supply and demand, due to the weak and pre-Keynesian nature of domestic European markets of that epoch[6] has nothing whatsoever to do with the Europe of today.

As for Joseph Schumpeter's political interpretation of imperialism, this is based on the militaristic, hierarchical, pre-democratic and pre-capitalist structures of some of the powers of that era and is thus not applicable to European liberal democracy.[7] Finally, although updated by 'dependency' theorists such as Theotonio Dos Santos and Samir

5. Desai, K. (2006). *The Inheritance of Loss.* Atlantic.
6. Hobson, J.A. (1902). *Imperialism: A Study.* New York: Pott. See also the analyses of Kemp, T. (1967). *Theories of Imperialism.* London: Dobson.
7. Schumpeter, J.A. (1918-19). "Zur Soziologie der Imperialismen", in *Archiv für Sozialwissnschaft und Sozialpolitik* XLVI: 1-39, 275-310.

Amin[8] in the 60s and 70s, the marxist developments of imperial theory by Lenin, Luxemburg and Bukharin, based on Hobson's analysis, had already revealed their analytical flaws in the inter-war years. This can be seen in the emergence of Gramsci's alternative notion of international 'hegemony', which focused on the emerging American power and on the epochal importance of 'Americanism.'[9] As for Wallerstein updating the dependence theory through the opposition centre-periphery (and the intermediary role of the semi-periphery) has recently produced a forecast of increasing conflict within the centre: between an emerging EU and declining US.[10]

In their book *Empire,* Toni Negri and Michael Hardt attempt to reconcile various metaphoric references to classic empires with a sociological analysis of the crisis of the state and contemporary politics (from Luhmann's systems theory to the many schools of postmodern thought that incorporate the idea of the decline of classic state power).[11] To what extent does the Hardt and Negri's concept of post-state, which attempts at recuperating and integrating neo-mediaevalist and post-modern literature, provide new theoretical insight in the debate? The decline of the modern state is interpreted as a possible end to state sovereignty *tout court*. Furthermore, such a mixture of the pre-modern and post-modern leads to the end of politics, either through the primacy of the economy and/or the competitive Foucault style, micro-powers within multilevel global governance. From this comes the functionalist and economistic and liberal idea of the radical 'deterritorialisation' of power. Just as Leninism and liberalism both paradoxically underestimated the expansive nature of new Keynesian capitalism, so too the postmodern heirs of Leninism are united with neoliberals in refusing to acknowledge the importance of the great international political game that has been taking place, particularly between western countries. The idea of a western world Leviathan,

8. These Latin-American and African scholars relaunched the economic theory of imperialism in the 1970s, highlighting the organic and un-reformable nature of Third World dependence with respect to the capitalist North. The decline of this theory, which had won considerable support both in the UN and in CEPAL, was in part due to the failure of economic policies of national 'disconnection' from world markets recommended to various governments.

9. Gramsci, A. (1975). "Americanismo e fordismo", *Quaderno 22*, edited by F. De Felice, Einaudi, Torino.

10. Wallerstein, I. (2006). *The Decline of US hegemony.*

11. Hardt, M. and A. Negri (2000). *Empire.* Cambridge, Mass.: Harvard University Press.

including economicaly centralised globalisation and political power, ignores the political limits of US power and the attempts of other states and regional powers as the EU to politically thwart hegemonic designs along with the geopolitical conflicts of interest between the US and other major capitalist countries, including its European allies.

What renders the metaphor of empire dated and caricatured, whether it is used to demonise or in apologia, is that such accounts ignore various signs of internal fragility[12] and political contradictions that are growing with unprecedented clarity. When they limit their study of the alternatives to empire to the 'revolt of the masses', Hardt and Negri forget that, rather than the 'neo-sorelian' myth of a 'revolt of the masses' resistance to unipolarist tendencies lies more in the emergence of a plurality of political actors and forces in the form either of single states (e.g. Brazil, China, India, Indonesia and Russia) in the new political dimension of regional groupings and in democratic public opinion. These are precisely the new political phenomena to which this book aims to draw attention, because they allow multilateral organisations to exist and act—whether in terms of opposing imperial tendencies of the superpower or exerting their right to act more independently from its particular priorities.[13]

It is worth dwelling a moment on the central concept of the postmodern, deterritorialised, borderless, eternal and global empire that is being hypothesised.[14] Of course, the functional, transnational and deterritorialised aspect of the empire exists. The strength of leading nations lies in their ability to synthesise the functional and territorial forms of domination and hegemony. In the current historical

12. Todd, E. (2002). *Après l'Empire. Essai sur la décomposition du système américain*. Paris: Gallimard.

13. The association of 'universal' multilateral organisations with the interests of the empire has been shattered by the conflicts the US has had in recent years with the United Nations, the WTO, the Kyoto Protocol and the International Criminal Court. The reference to Kelsen is interesting, albeit excessive (pp.45-89), given that today we are witnessing the exact opposite—a qualitative and quantitative increase in the political contradictions between American globalism and an international system of justice.

14. The theory of the redundancy of the historic and spatial-temporal dimension is analogous here to Fukuyama's liberal ideology (see *The End of History op. cit.*). See also Hardt and Negri, *Empire op. cit.:* 21-37. Its criticism of Arrighi, and especially of Wallerstein and the idea of cycles of power, highlights this regression (pp. 225-27). In support of the theory of hegemonic cycles, see Gilpin, R. (1981). *War and Change in World Politics*. London : Cambridge University Press, and Taylor, P.J. (2002). "The American Century as Hegemonic Cycle", in P.K. O'Brien and A. Clesse (eds.), *Two Hegemonies. Britain 1846-1914 and the United States 1941-2001*. Ashgate, Aldershot. pp.284-302.

phase, these are framed by a strategic design of a world order that reorganises geographical spaces and technical forms of strategic and military presence.[15] These also include protectionist policies such as agricultural and steel subsidies designed to satisfy domestic electoral requirements.

The notion and practice of sovereignty is opposing the US and the EU, which cannot be considered as part of a unique centre. Two main arguments can be played for this purpose. Firstly, the current contradictions on a global level explain why Robert Keohane, with regard to George W. Bush's United States, referred with a certain irony to classic political and territorial sovereignty, in contrast to any post-modern notion of Empire. It is perhaps surprising to find a country that, unlike states in Europe, was the product of the federalist idea of shared sovereignty, but which is now re-launching important aspects of the classic image of the great power in terms of how it conceives of and manages its foreign policy and spheres of influence[16] (e.g. Afghanistan and Iraq). The US obsession for a territorial interpretation of a trans-national phenomenon is so strong that it comes at the price of disastrous inefficiencies in the battle against informal terrorism. Contrary to post-modern theories, the territorial dimension matters. The shortcomings of postmodernism demonstrate the need to understand institutionalism not as simply opposed to realism but as a possible positive 'overcoming' of the best legacies of realism, while openly criticising its updated version. The various meanings of the expression 'deterritorialised empire' therefore only highlight the

15. See Czempiel's analysis of the costly global reorganisation of the US military presence (Weltpolitik im Umbruch *op. cit.:* 144-62). Indeed, on the geopolitical front, the US with its 36,000 troops stationed in Europe is seeking to gain greater influence over Eastern Europe through NATO. It has politicised the FTAA project in Latin America and implanted itself in the Middle East with 139,000 troops in Iraq and a further 20,000 in other countries in the area. It maintains a military presence in central Asia and Afghanistan (10,000 troops) and flanks China, from the 31,000 troops in South Korea to its base at Okinawa. We should also not forget that the 7th fleet and the APEC project guarantee its presence in the Asia-Pacific region—the 'American lake'. A new initiative regarding Africa would complete the geopolitical picture. On the strategic level, the US is interested in a) securing new bases outside Europe and Japan, to allow greater flexibility in organising attack forces; b) gaining access to new lines of command for military training; c) reorganising its attack forces and hardware, corresponding to its varying objectives of regional dissuasion; d) improving mobility, in order to be capable of launching long-range military attacks on targets armed with WMD (Department of Defence, *Quadrennial Defence op. cit.:* 26).

16. Keohane, R.O. (2003). "Ironies of Sovereignty: The EU and the US", in J.H.H. Weiler, I. Begg and J. Eterson (eds.), *Integration in an Expanding European Union. Reassessing the Fundamentals.* Malden (Mass.): Blackwell. pp. 307-30.

difficulty in interpreting the present reality without recourse to the categories of the past. Even if refined in a syncretic sense, it remains so obsolete and imprecise a term that it does not stand up to empirical or theoretical scrutiny. Let's conclude by emphasising the current EU and India roles, in limiting US hard power. Regarding the EU, the "Habermas notion" of "divided west" includes the practical transatlantic rift, the geopolitical differences as interest are concerned, the opposed external expectations as the respective roles of the EU and US are concerned. All in all, Europe shows an alternative international image: we will focus on the European interregional, bilateral, multilateral relations and their 'mirror effect' on EU international identity.

Second, the nature of the internal polity matters. Like the Indian federation, the EU is based on the principle of shared sovereignty and that keeps it relevant in the 21st century. As far as Europe is concerned, the theoretical background of shared sovereignty is deeply rooted in the history of Western political thought against the idea of despotism and tyranny. Even absolutist European theories of State power imply to some extent "limits of power." Machiavelli's state (*Prince*, 1513), is a concentration of force. However, in the "Art of War" the European distinctive 'virtus', thanks to the variety of states and republics and to their balance implies that states cooperation makes the absolute liberty of states limited and embedded and. Bodin's (*Six books on the Republic*, 1576) theory of sovereignty, mentions however limits of sovereignty (natural law and private property of families).

Hobbes (1641) describes the state as a "Leviathan"; however, absolute power is paradoxically based on voluntary contract, on rational choice of individuals. Two constitutional traditions of "shared power" as self limitation of power emerges in Europe in the 18th century: the double Federalist tradition on the one hand: Althusius, Montesquieu, and, as a consequence, the US "federalist papers" (1787); Kant's (1795 and 1793) critics of both, state sovereignty and of 'universal monarchy' (empire) and the theory of peace based on three pre-conditions: federalism, republicanism and cosmopolitanism. On the other hand, the tradition of the so-called mixed government: in that case, stability and good government are better provided by combined principles: democracy, aristocracy, monarchy (Polibius, Cicero, Montesquieu, Hegel, Bobbio), which today means, democratic, technocratic and diplomatic principles.

Both traditions make of the "shared power" a solid pillar underpinning the EU *longue durée* institution building during more than 50 years as pointed out among others by R.O. Keohane (2003): "Ironies of sovereignty", opposing the EU to the US new assertive international power. Despite the stagnating explicit constitutionalisation process, the EU shows a consolidated praxis of shared power: pooling and sharing sovereignty; supranational institutions and consensual management of national diversities; an implicit constitutionalisation process, since 1950 (Treaty of Paris) and 1957 (Treaty of Rome). The consequence of this internal institution building on external action is that never could the EU act as a classical, unitarian, assertive, rapid, State, namely in declaring and implementing war.

Balveer Arora's analysis of the Indian state provides an excellent background for comparative research on the distinctive link between internal polity and foreign policy. Even if India, contrary to the EU, is a State indeed, the Presidential and Parliamentary system looks unable to effectively work as an "Imperial presidency", as Schlesinger defined the centralising US decision making process.

Civilian Powers and New Multilateralism

Coming back to the features of the globalising world of the early 21st century, the divided West is part of a transitional post-1989 world which is characterised by what Raimond Aron called an "heterogeneous international system." Unipolar tendencies are limited and balanced by both multipolar and multilateral tendencies. By multipolar we mean the option asserted by nuclear power Russia and, to a lesser extent, by a Chinese Republic minimising its growing stature. By multilateral tendency we mean the will of strengthening inter-state cooperation as a priority of foreign policy. Not only "European security strategy,"[17] but also several other counties and regional entities are oriented to new concepts of foreign policy linked to "human security"

17. European Council (2003). *A Secure Europe in a Better World*, European Security Strategy. December (often called "Solana paper").

multilateral perspectives[18] and that in spite of September 11th and the increasing militarisation of the international agenda by the US administration: for example the case of Japan ("Freedom from want"[19]), Canada ("Freedom from Fear"[20]), Brazil/Argentina (joint renunciation to the nuclear armaments in name of the NPT and of the building of a regional security community, MERCOSUR), international organisation as the OCDE and the UNDP and of India. The civilian power idea is a relevant part of such a new multilateral culture and tendency. My understanding of civilian power takes into account the impact of ideas, knowledge, law and other factors in underpinning a new notion of cooperative power. Neither the EU nor India can be considered as classical military powers, whether we consider that a good or bad thing. Will they become such a classical power in the future? Indian nuclear armament and the EU rapid reaction force (decided at the Helsinki European council of 1999) look contradictory to the notion of civilian power only for superficial observers.

We already mentioned a first structural reason making it impossible for the EU to move to a military power model: its internal polity. A second one should be quoted. It is the so called "European way of life", defined as a "European Dream" by J. Rifkin, and in more appropriate terms, "European social model" by both J. Habermas and the European council of Lisbon (March 2000), making impossible for every political leader including Berlusconi, Chirac, Blair to dramatically change the national budget, cutting welfare and fostering a national defence budget. European States spend, on an average, between 1 and 2 per cent of their GSP for defence while the US and China, spend 3.3 per cent (420 billions dollars and 43 billions dollars respectively in 2006) The further obstacle is, since 1997 (treaty of Amsterdam) a legal one: the EU external action can be implemented only within the limits of the Treaty framework of the so-called "Petersberg tasks" that is humanitarian intervention peace keeping missions and peace

---

18. Paris, R. (2001). "Human Security :paradigm shift or Hot Air ?" in *International Security* 26: 87-102 and Remacle, E. (2007). *Human Security, Origins and Political Use of a Foreign Policy.* Concept Paper. School in EU Studies, ULB.

19. Fukushima, A. (1999). *Japanese Foreign Policy.* London: Macmillan.

20. Axworthy, L. (1997). "Canada and Human Security", *International Journal:* 183-84 and E. Remacle and S. Jaumain (2006). *Mémoire de guerre et construction de la paix.* Belgique, Europe, Canada: Peter Lang Bruxelles.

enforcing missions; nothing else. With this background to talk about the militarisation of EU power is nonsensical. India also cannot be qualified as a classical military power: the first reason is the reduced military budget and the only local/regional scope of its nuclear weapons (aimed at balancing Pakistani nuclear armament). Secondly, the country's political culture is not only democratic and federalist but also pacifist: the evolution from Mahatma Gandhi's political thought[21] to a modern Indian understanding of power is more complex than a simple and trivial move from idealism to realism. Continuity matters as well as discontinuity. As for the above mentioned link between modern political thought and the current EU, the *longue durée* legacy of Mahatma Gandhi and Nehru is still a decisive reference for understanding the nature of Indian foreign policy and international identity. History matters more than governments.

But, if neither India and the EU are now, nor can become in the future, classical military kind of powers, should we import the US notion of "soft power" or recover the idealistic notion of "gentle power" to understand their international roles? We do not think so. We do not share the caricatural opposition by Robert Kagan of Venus (EU) and Mars (US). Neither is the more sophisticated plea of J. Nye of being a soft power appropriate for the EU and India. What we need is to go beyond the simple opposition between Nye's notion of "soft power", as balancing hard power in the context of the evolution of a classical power (which might be appropriated for the example of US power) on the one hand; and, on the other hand, the idealistic notion of civil power as a kind of "civilising power", which looks dominant in the pioneer reflection of F. Duchêne and has been recently relaunched by several scholars (EU as a gentle power, as a normative model for global governance, EU as norm setting power, and so on...) is not fit to cope with the current nature of European and Indian powers.

In my opinion the first concept is much affected by the classical notion of power, combining *"Macht"* and *"Herrschaft"* in the Max Weber understanding (even if oscillating between hard and soft power, according to the outcomes of domestic elections). So, even if it provides empirical inputs for comparative research (Nye, 2004; 2005)

---

21. Fischer, Louis (1954). *Gandhi*. Penguin and Mentor Books.

it is completely unfit to account for an entity such as the EU or a polity such as India. As the second concept is concerned, it is dominated by one of the following theoretical backgrounds: the cosmopolitan view of civilising powers as a step toward a pyramid kind of peaceful world order, where the UN; by the post modern understanding of the decline of the sovereign state and the creation of a "post-westphalian" global community (Mastanduno, 2000); by the neo-medievalist notion of '*rétraite* of state' (Strange, 1995) and emerging multidimensional and multivelel "global governance without government"(Rosenau, 1992) . None of these concepts, are fit to cope with the reality of the post September 11th 2001 world. These theoretical perspectives were perhaps applicable in the optimistic environment of the nineties but are dramatically challenged by events and processes of the new century, changing the internal and external context of the European construction: Sept 11th 2001, the new US security strategy (2002-2005), the resilience of states.

Are Actually Civilian Powers Political Realities?

Is the European experiment relevant for India? And, vice versa, is India growing up as an economic and political power relevant for Europe? It is exactly what I'm looking for by my 'realist' interpretation of civilian power. It consists of five main features, combining the inside and outside dimensions and concretely challenging the classical notion of international power. Only the last one can be characterised as being of a normative nature.

1) *Internal foreign policy*. After 1945 the European international identity has been increasingly characterised as being oriented towards internal conflict prevention and settlement. Where is the hard core of what Karl Deutsch called a "security community"?

   According to Jürgen Habermas: "you can never underestimate the salience of the French-German reconciliation"(*Divided West*, 2004). Does established peace between former enemies entail a dynamic meaning for the 21st century? It is a matter of facts that EU cooperation and integration as a means towards pacification and democratisation has been able to spread beyond the limits of the western European hard core and to include the continent. This work in progress is the main EU contribution towards global governance. The problem is that, while in the first decades such an extraordinary legacy was strong enough to provide the EC with a "substantial legitimacy" it reveals itself as insufficient in the 21st century. The decline of memory of past wars and fears of a too quickly widening EU plays a role in affecting this "*acquis*". However, it still matters as a hard core of EU cooperation and integration at a continental level and as a concrete example of conflict prevention for troubled regions elsewhere. The widening process is a crucial part of the updating of such a distinctive feature: For example, research on the background of the criteria of Copenhagen for enlargement (democracy, rule of law and social market economy) proves the constructivist interpretation of the effective weight of the ideal variable (for discourse, ideas etc, see *Rhetorical Entrapment,* by Schimmelfenning). It is important to underline that the EU is a civilian power also because the majority of MS are civilian powers: the weight of history and memory in founding international responsibility, pacifism, commitment to North South cooperation, are still effective foreign policy drivers for many MS, namely Germany, Italy, Austria, Scandinavia, the Iberian and Benelux countries, and elsewhere.

Is this experience relevant for Asia? Certainly for East Asia where the 20th century tragic history still represents a huge inter-state problem, especially since it is an uncomfortable truth for Japan. And what about India? Even the Indian subcontinent has had many past wars and tragedies linked to the Kashmir issue, had to be overcome by increasing states cooperation and people to people understanding: the India-Pakistan reconciliation being the main issue at stake. Without a constructive neighbourhood policy, good relations with Islamic countries of the area, conflict setting, India and others will be compelled to rearm thereby threatening their development and modernisation policies. So, as in Europe, Latin America, South East-Asia, regional cooperation is the best framework for preventing and managing border conflicts, settling minority problems.

In conclusion, supporting dialogue at the level of civil societies, and strengthening SAARC, looks to many observers as the way to balance the internal asymmetry of the subcontinent between a rising India and its neighbours, by networking of social actors, institutionalising of rules, and procedures, and implementing common policies.

2) *Various national backgrounds are underpinning the EU as a "cooperative power"*. The Inter-governmental bargaining could be interpreted as a gradual civilisation of national sovereignties even if there are problems and difficulties in institutional settlement and in the pooling in and sharing of sovereignties. On the basis of successful collective internal governance (Wallace, Wallace and Pollack, 2005), a cooperative power acts as a distinctive multilateral player, strengthening international regimes, asserting foreign relations based on a dynamic balance between short term national interest and construction of inter-state trust. Regional regimes of cooperation between states cannot become united political systems everywhere; however the actual EU-27 path is more modest and communicative, managing national diversities towards increasing socio-economic convergence.

3) *Civilian power as a power of knowledge and internal social cohesion.* Where are to be found the resources of external power in the 21st century global world? The "Lisbon agenda" (2000-2010), notwithstanding the very well known problems, very well shows how relevant the issue of the balance between social justice and economic modernisation is in Europe. Chinese, Indian, and Brazilian policy makers wish for a dialogue on the same.[22] B. Arora and other Indian intellectuals showed interest in such an experiment. Its external dimension should not be neglected. Not only does the Lisbon agenda provide a possible collective answer to globalisation, but it is an active component

22. An international conference on the external dimension of the Lisbon agenda has been organised by the IEEI of Lisbon on March 1st 2007.

of EU/EC external relations: research, and cooperation policy. Europe and India accept the global market but that does not mean denying the need for searching distinctive ways to a knowledge society. Diversities belong to the past but is the global convergence balanced by national and regionalist trends, a distinctive reaction to the impact of the same global market? We guess that a pluralistic understanding of globalisation includes national patterns towards socio-economic modernisation and a non-technocratic understanding of convergence, benchmarking and technological innovation.

The "Galileo satellite recognition project", "Airbus", "Ariane space research" etc are interesting empirical examples to be investigated. India's service based-economy, a society where ICT is a key sector of the economy, may provide further examples of the external relevance of cooperative international power based on knowledge, technology and economic growth. How do we reconcile such huge achievements with the challenges typical of a classic developing country? Despite progress in reducing poverty, social discrepancies are still impressive, $2/3^{rd}$ of the population are still employed in agriculture, 400 million people earn less than 1 dollar a day, which makes for a very low per-capita GDP (720 dollars compared with 1740 in China). The level of education and health care are extremely poor, and the fiscal policy is still totally ineffective, in short, India is ranked as 126th out of the 186 world states as far as human development is concerned (UN data 2006). The digital divide is also shown by there being only 7 million Internet users. The "structural power" concept of S. Strange is relevant: social cohesion and knowledge are seen as resource of power which may matter more than the military. The "Lisbon agenda" set in 2000 has launched the common objective of building an "European Knowledge society consistent with our values and aims of social cohesion." This objective is relevant for India too: social cohesion, infrastructure-building, fighting social exclusion, development access to ICT beyond the current digital divide, may create resources for external relations and foreign policy, more effective than nuclear power.

4) *Structural Foreign Policy*. The European Union tends to have a structural foreign policy in that it aims at affecting 'particularly the economic and social structures of partners (states, regions, economic actors, international organisations, etc.), and the context wherein they act. This kind of foreign policy is implemented through long term, mainly pacific and original means (diplomatic relations, agreements, sanctions and so on), and its scope is not conjunctural but rather in the middle and long range'. Namely: a) multidimensional external relations changing the environment where the state and private actors behave (trade policy, cooperation with developing countries, humanitarian aid etc); b) bilateral relations (conditionality) pushing partners to democratise and cooperate at the regional level (in Eastern Europe pre-accession strategies); d) inter-regionalism as a new feature of international relations between bilateralism and global multilateralism; e) cultural dialogue as a piecemeal contribution to an alliance between civilisations. Several structural foreign policies result in supporting regional cooperation elsewhere as a way of limiting international anarchy (Waltz, Kenneth. *Theory of International Politics,* 1979).

5) *Civilian power as norms setting actor at regional and global level: A perennial of the history of political thought*. To what extent could international life be partially democratised and submitted to legal norms, beyond mere power relations? The concept of "normative power" is an attempt to suggest that not only is the EU constructed on a normative basis, but importantly that this predisposes it to act in a normative way in world politics. Of course, the link with the previous points is crucial: it is built on the crucial, and usually overlooked observation, that the most important factor shaping the international role of the EU is not what it does or what it says, but what it is.' (Manners, 2002: 252). We need an exchange of "cognitive models" as Umberto Eco says: the Gandhian idea of trusteeship, the value of non-possession, means that "we, as individuals, institutions and groups are embedded in something larger than ourselves. The fragile ecosystem is crying for a new world politics based in part upon the idea of

trusteeship."[23] Second, may the regional role of India within the unstable and, from a democratic point of view, fragile subcontinent be enhanced? Could SAARC play a role of stabiliser of domestic democracy in the region? In the area of democratisation, the EU has been an active agent in the provision of election assistance and observation and has recently developed guidelines that go towards the principles of good governance. In the area of human rights, the EU has developed a pro-active policy of being at the vanguard of the abolitionist movement against capital punishment and the death penalty, particularly striking in the aftermath of the end of the Cold War. The role of the EU founding values should also be quoted, and their consistency with UN Charta as well. Implications on the EU international political identity are obvious.

New Theoretical Challenges

The innovative perspective described above is however submitted to some relevant and challenging caveats which cannot be ignored:

a) *First caveat:* Is it possible to construct a theory of international power based only on a single case study? Of course, it is not. The new era of EU studies should go beyond inward looking theories of integration or traditional focus on comparative federalism US-EU and rather include a comparative analysis of an alternative kind of power elsewhere and of India's international role as well. What we need is first of all more comparative research on new emerging civilian powers and regional actors abroad; in Latin America, South Asia and Africa. To what extent, do national actors and regional regimes evolve towards neighbouring state cooperation towards self-limitation of national sovereignty and the incipient building up of transnational political systems? Can regional cooperation help by stabilising domestic democracies? What balance between exogenous and endogenous factors is possible in explaining peaceful regional cooperation?

---

23. Varun Shani (Jawaharlal Nehru University. New Delhi) mentioned this concept as a possible distinctive voice of India in the future. See "Coping with Hegemony: Is There an Indian Way?". Transcultura Conference. Brussels. November 2006.

b) *Second caveat.* Coping with neorealist challenges after the emergence of the terrorist threat, and the new US security agenda is a must. We need new international relations research on evolving post-cold war global system focusing on the following issue: after the coming back of security as a central issue of international relations what about a serious, realistic foundation of multilateralism, not as a mere system of governance but as a world order, distinct respectively from multipolarism, unipolarism and anarchy? It is a matter of a process of change occurring within a global process of change. India and the EU should work on this agenda.

c) *Third caveat.* Inside/outside ironies of democracy. To what extent is the consolidation of democratic and civilian powers in the new century strongly affected by the decreasing legitimacy of the institutions of global and regional governance? There is no evidence that the current internal legitimacy crisis of the EU will have consequences on external relations. Output legitimacy is crucial: success of external missions, efficiency of decision making, concrete outcomes as the successful management of world emergencies as poverty, pollution, peace, epidemic diseases...However, the legitimacy crisis may have a major impact since the link between external credibility and internal democratic performance is obvious. The declining input legitimacy, lacking coherences, double standards, ineffectiveness (of failure to show effectiveness) all threaten external credibility, with significant repercussions both on the near and far abroad. In conclusion: which relationship between national civilian powers, regional regimes and democracy, both as stabilisation of domestic democracy and democratisation of the global system.?

d) *Which possible combination is possible between multipolarism and multilateralism?* India, like France, China and Russia, has a positive understanding of multipolarism, while the EU is more cautious. However, in case of a multipolar world, coming back to power politics would be inevitable. India would be used by the USA to counterbalance China. In our opinion, even during the BJP government of Vajpajee the Indian tradition of pacifism political thought, the Nehruvian legacy was able to survive and military concept of multipolarism was not popular enough.[24] After the US-India rapprochement, the objective of simply realigning India as part of a US-led containment of China (whose other pieces are the strengthened links of the US with Japan, the Japan-Australia alliance, the support to Taiwan and Pakistan, and US troops in central Asia), has been openly contrasted by the dramatic and promising improvement of India-China relations in 2005-06 (visits to New Dehli of Prime Minister Wen Jinbao in 2005 and President Hu Jin-Tao in 2006). In this time of a restructuring of India's foreign policy, the EU and the world should look with sympathy towards India for proving and asserting in new terms its autonomy. Sending of wrong or oscillating messages to China could provoke security dilemmas, re-armament and instability in the region and beyond. The multilateral and bilateral engagement of China looks successful so far. Through the dialogue, India could to some extent represent and foster the democratic future of China, because it realised democracy before full development. Something like that could be attempted in the case of Iran also. What is going to become crucial is the will of transforming bilateral arrangements into steps towards strengthening of, and mutual coordination between, multilateral regimes and organisations, SAARC, WTO, ILO, UN and, last but not the least, The International Atomic Energy Agency (IAEA), Nuclear Suppliers Group (NSG), and so on.

All in all, the EU and India cannot be pacifist and post-modern islands surrounded by a hard Westphalian world. They need their strategic partnership to be deepened within a general revision of international relations of the new century. The key theoretical challenge for both partners is: which new multilateral framework could take stock of the progress and potentialities of European and Indian cooperation and avoid the dangers of unipolarism and of a multipolar nuclearised world? New multilateralism is the only possible

24. Chaulia, Sreeram, S. (2002-03). "BJP, India's Foreign Policy and the Realist Alternative", in *International Politics* 39(2): 215-234.

common framework for new practices of power to grow up. It should include the following conditions: increasing role of trans-national public opinion and centrality of the issue of human rights and legitimacy of global governance; a growing room for regional cooperation and associations between neighbouring states; more efficiency by facing the global emergencies (poverty, peace, pollution, energy...). Of course, the role of the EU, India, but also of Japan, China, Brazil, Canada and other emerging actors is crucial by strengthening the global and regional regulating framework and building up new multilateral regimes: ICC, Kyoto Protocol...as a framework for new bilateral partnerships, including the one between the EU-India.

References

Manners, Ian (2002). "Normative Power Europe: A Contradiction in Terms?", in *Journal of Common Market Studies* 40(2): 252.

Mastanduno, Michael and Gene M. Lyons (eds.) (1995). *Beyond Westphalia?*. Baltimore: Johns Hopkins University Press.

Nye, Joseph S. (2002). *The Paradox of American Power*. New York: Oxford University Press.

———. (2004). *Soft Power: The Means to Success on World Politics*. New York: Palgrave.

Rosenau, J.N. and E-O Czempiel (eds.) (1992). *Governance without Government: Order and Change in World Politics*. Cambridge: Cambridge University Press.

Strange, S. (1996). *The Retreat of State: The Diffusion of Power in the World Economy*. Cambridge: Cambridge University Press.

Wallace, Helen, William Wallace and M. Pollack (eds.) (2005). *Policy-making in the EU*. Oxford University Press.

7

Identity Configurations in India-Europe Relations

SHAZIA AZIZ WÜLBERS

Introduction

This paper is part of my doctoral thesis in which I try to argue that EU India relations are not working particularly well, in spite of all the efforts made by both sides. In my thesis I deal with political relations, economic relations, aid and development and cultural relations. The present paper is a part of my chapter on EU-India cultural relations, where I try to make the point that the images and representations that India has of the EU and vice versa do not correspond to the reality and cause friction between the two. India would like to be seen as the new emerging political and economic power even if the current reality maybe that it's a very fast growing developing country and on the other hand, the European Union would like to be seen as an important political and normative actor, even if right now, it is not seen as one. Both are victims of stereotyping and prejudices, which have a strong impact on the actual potential of their interaction.

I have chosen the Mittal-Arcelor deal as an example par excellence of these identity clashes which are based on constructed identities of the 'other' and hinder meaningful exchanges.

The Conceptual Framework

Identity is the set of characteristics belonging to an individual or shared by all members of the group. These identities become apparent or nurture themselves in relation to 'others'. They are not a static phenomena but are developed through a continuous process of identification.

In an ideal world, identities would be describing individuals or groups as a whole but in our practical and real world, identities are formed with past memories, present situations and of course, fears of the future and of the unknown. In essence, these identities are formed as a result of interactions between the 'self' and 'others' and most importantly with the interpretations of each others signals. Thus identities are truly dynamic and interactive. The important point to be made here is that usually we choose a few attractive features of our culture as elements of our self image and a few less attractive features of 'other cultures'.[1] And this ends up playing a role in causing conflict situations.

Knowing that individuals and groups posses multiple and changing identities, makes identity studies an extremely formidable subject to study. I have chosen to study the changing identities of Indians and Europeans through a concrete case study of the Mittal Arcelor deal. Through this paper I have researched on how the clash of these identities played a role in trade negotiations and corporate deals.

Postmodernists insist that identities are constructed and inculcated into societies and I fully agree with this. Some 20 years ago, Indian politicians and civil society were predominant with pleas for international aid because of the precarious situation of the Indian economy and the public. However, now, it's the same India which refused Tsunami aid from Western countries, insisting that it was capable of dealing with the victims. The change in identity is phenomenal. Needless to say, an India expecting to be treated as an equal, tends to overreact when the treatment received is below the expectations engendered by its newly acquired identity.

Although, India is still classified as a developing country, Indians have been quick to profit from the globalising world and would like to be treated as equals. This change in identity has happened over the past 10-15 years, where India experienced a consistent high growth rate. Indian ventures have increased manifold over these years and they have made efforts to forge new ties and deals with the rest of the world, in lieu of its growing status. The latest Indo-US deal is the "cherry on the cake."

India regards itself as the third world leader and Indians feel

1. This point is very well made by Mach, Zdzislaw (1993). *Symbols, Conflict and Identity*. New York: New York State University Press. p.7.

considerable national pride in that. The "image of a prosperous industrialised India, which could defeat the West at its own game"[2] seems very real.

To the Indians chagrin, the world is not reacting fast enough to their brand new identity of a booming economy.

The reason behind this slow reaction may be buried deep in European history books. Since time immemorial, India was the 'other' in Eurocentric world history.

Western philosophers, in their lengthy accounts of the caste system have kept India ancient in the eyes of Europeans. And interesting work has been done by Ronald Inden[3] who has tried to understand why India was always considered non materialistic, non rational and highly spiritual. He suggests that writers have used soft metaphors[4] for India that continue to impact the present European mind. The earlier European writer decided that the way to study India was through religion, and their religion of choice was Hinduism. In the early 20th Century, Indian authors themselves spoke against British Utilitarianism and glorified Hinduism,[5] adding to the bulk of already existing literature on India and Hinduism.

Consequently, for a long time, European identity was constructed on the basis of a strong superiority complex, regarding, Europeans as rational and scientific and the 'others' including Indians, as irrational and imaginative.

However, this superiority complex suffered a strong blow in the aftermath of the Second World War, with the horrors of the holocaust and the barbaric nature of some fellow Europeans being revealed. In addition to that, the Second World War heralded a new era in history,

---

2. Bannerjee, Ashis (1989). "The Ideology and Politics of India's National Identity" in Zoya Hasan *et al.* (ed.), *The State Political Process and Identity: Reflections on Modern India.* New Delhi: Sage Publications. pp.283-96.

3. His book tries to reconstruct Indian history to show its true modernity. The book is entitled, *"Imagining India,"* Oxford: Basil Blackwell. 1990.

4. India as a female, Indian thought as a dream, caste society as a centrifuge, Hinduism as a jungle or a sponge etc.

5. Please refer to this article for the rise of Hindu Nationalism in India, written by Jaffrelot, Christophe (2001). "The Rise of Hindu Nationalsim and the marginalisation of Muslims in India Today" in Amita Shastri and A. Jeyatratnam Wilson (eds.), *The Post-colonial States of South Asia: Democracy, Identity, Development and Security*, Richmond: Curzon Press. pp.141-157.

where the centre of power and influence shifted to the United States and the Soviet Union.[6]

A new identity was in the making, and still is, in many ways. In the case of Europe, there are probably two identities going parallel to one other and sometimes clashing among themselves and creating conflict. The identity of being European and sharing a common European history, which was a world power before but now is relegated to being second after the US and the identity of being a part of the European Union, which is actively competing with the US and other global players in the world.

The Arcelor Mittal conflict came right in the middle of these two conflicting European identities and the newly formed Indian identity based on India's latest economic successes and development.

The Arcelor Mittal Controversy

On January 27, 2006, Lakshmi Mittal made a bid of $22 billion for the European steel giant, Arcelor. The bid was classified as 'hostile' and the board of directors rejected it outright. Mittal steel company was the largest steel company by volume and aspired to be the one with the largest turnover in the world. If the deal was to go through it would increase by three times the steel output and profit margins of the company. The two companies would complement each other, since Mittal Steels has markets in the US and Eastern Europe and Arcelor is a major player in the West European and South American markets.

From the outset, there was sharp resistance from Arcelor. And as events unfolded, it smelt more of 'undisguised racism',[7] rather than corporate rivalry. The French Chief Executive Officer (CEO) of Arcelor called Mittal a less than average businessman and called the steel he made *eau de cologne* as compared to the real French perfume made by

6. For more details on European Identity, please refer to Frank, Robert (1999). "European Identities, Consciousness and Construction: Harmony and Disharmony between Politics, Economics and Integration" in H.S Chopra *et al.* (ed.), *National Identity and Regional Cooperation: Experiences of European Integration and South Asian Perspectives*. New Delhi: Manohar Publications. pp. 43-58.

7. Gow, David (2006). "Race to dominate", in *The Guardian: Economic Dispatch*. February 02. on the internet address of *http://business.guardian.co.uk/economicdispatch/story/0,,1700852,00.html*

Arcelor! For the first time such a large company, led by an Indian, with a new and different business model[8] was posing a threat and a challenge to a strong European company. European companies who turned to India and China for cheap labour were challenged by an Indian for take-over. The change in situation was rather drastic and painful. There was a time when big multinational companies had to be either European or American.

This new reality and this new change in identity of Indians is hard to comprehend and to adjust to. Europeans, being rather normative in their approach till now, had to deal with a change in their identity as well. Europeans who had dictated ways to the 'others' had to adjust to the idea of being taken over by an Indian. The spiritual and exotic Indian had turned into a shrewd and rich businessman.

After about three months of over reaction by the European and Indian media, on the 19th of May, Mittal increased his bid by 38.7per cent to $32.5 billion. In the meanwhile, French, Spanish and Luxemburg politicians and labour unions lashed out at Mittal, being worried about job losses, in spite of reassurances from Lakshmi Mittal who explained that none of his previous takeovers had involved job cuts. These countries concerns are understandable since they have the largest work force share of Arcelor and such big mergers, almost always end up in job cuts.

The Indian government made efforts to clinch this deal which developed a racist tinge and was insulting to the new Indian identity, where Indians wanted to be treated on par with Europeans. The *Financial Times* claimed that the Indian government threatened to not ratify the double taxation accord between it and Luxembourg, if the Luxembourg government did not lower its resistance.[9] Kamal Nath, Indias's Trade Minister, went to the extent of calling these attacks xenophobic.

Arcelor attempted to make a deal with a Russian company, Severstal but this move was rejected by Arcelor's shareholders, when it was submitted to the vote. According to Colette Neuville, who

---

8. Giridharadas, Anand (2006). "Europe's fear of pinstriped Indians" in *International Herald Tribune*. Mumbai edition. February 03.

9. "Covert India threat got Mittal the deal" in *Financial Times*, Front Page, June 30th 2006.

represents small shareholders, the Arcelor board of directors acted against the interests of the company and its shareholders.[10] It is widely assumed that Guy Dolle's tactics to avoid collaborating with Mittal Steels went beyond any corporate logic.

On the 25th of June, The Mittal Arcelor deal came through, by far the most controversial and publicised corporate take-over in recent corporate history.

When the deal was struck, it was widely applauded by the Indian press, and it was even compared to a legend.[11] It was acclaimed as a triumph over 'European Prejudices' and racism.

The fact of the matter is that Lakshmi Mittal is a clever business man and knew how to stir some Indian government officials and the Indian media. He provoked knowingly or unknowingly an identity conflict between both sides.

Analysis of the Turn of Events

This five month saga was an important event to understand the complexities of intercultural interactions.

Firstly, the most important reason for this conflict was not a clash of civilisations as proclaimed by the Indian press but a complex clash of newly developing identities and the lack of the other group appreciating them.

This deal was an example, par excellence of clashing identities. Some of the European politicians and Arcelor dealt with India, personified by Mittal in this case by Indian politicians and the media, using the old European approach of the 'other'. Even if they had been aware of India's economic rise, the basic idea that has been inculcated in them through years of historical writings could not be so easily washed away.

But the fact that Arcelor shareholders decided to vote for the merger is a ray of hope. It could be argued that usually the shareholders major concerns are the value of his shares and the

---

10. Naravane, Vaiju (2006). "Mittal wins over Arcelor" in *The Hindu*, Front Page. 30th June.
11. Swapan Dasgupta refers to the Mittal triumph as "the stuff that legends are made of" in his article entitled, "Mulling over Mittal" in The Telegraph, 30th June 2006.

"colour of the skin" of the head of the company. Going by this logic, the board of directors should have had the same preoccupation. The shareholders, in accepting the Mittal offer, proved that India's changing self identity had had an impact in European eyes.

Moreover, there were two different forces working at a tangent to each other, which added to the controversy. The European Union, with its normative characters proved to be better placed in dealing with the Indian government and Laksmi Mittal than some of the concerned member states.

The European Union played an extremely positive role in trying to dissipate the crisis.[12] Kamal Nath, India's Commerce and Industry Minister sent a letter to European Trade Commissioner Peter Mandelson to complain about the European governments who were, according to him, breaking WTO rules of "national treatment"[13] and that their stiff opposition amounted to xenophobia. The EU Commissioner for internal trade, Charlie McCreevy, insisted that the stands taken by some European governments were contrary to the spirit of the rules on free movement of capital. He expressed concern about the 'poison pill.'[14] And David O Sullivan, European Commission Director General for trade, was quick to reiterate that commercial merits were more important than nationality and that the European Commission was going to keep a close eye on unfolding events and would punish immediately any violations of competition laws.[15]

Peter Mandelson, the EU Trade Commissioner and Jose Manuel

---

12. The accounts of Indian Newspapers about EU mediation are extremely interesting to study, since the Indian media has showed much more openness and understanding concerning the different identities of the European Union and the individual member countries. Please refer to the article titled "Mittal's Arcelor bid: EU against racial discrimination", *The Hindu*. 14th February 2006.

13. National Treatment means giving others the same treatment as one's own nationals. More details can be found on this rule by refereeing to the WTO website *http://www.wto.org/English/thewto_e/whatis_e/tif_e/fact2_e.htm*

14. Poison pill is the change of legislation by governments to avoid takeover by a foreign company. In the case of the Mittal deal, the French and Luxembourg governments considered this option. This option would mean that these governments would change a bill, through which the company board, under hostile pressure can take the liberty of deciding on its own, without direct consultation with shareholders. All this is because, if the shareholder is asked, they usually say yes to a lucrative offer, without caring about the colour of the skin!

15. In an article posted at the Deutsche Welle News channel on the internet address of *http://dwelle.de/southasia/india/1.171630.1.html*

Borroso, President of the European Commission, made several statements speaking against 'economic nationalism' of some individual member states.

Surprisingly enough, the Indian Prime Minister's Office and the Ministry of External Affairs did their level best to cool off the heat from this case and to stop this crisis spilling over and spoiling diplomatic relations between India and the European Union and also with individual countries. Anand Sharma, Minister of State for External Affairs, told journalists in a press conference to exercise restraint on blowing the issue out of proportions.

The whole logic of the new EU India strategic relationship came alive with this deal where both sides didn't let events take disproportionate shape and continued dialogue during the storm. However, this in essence, is also an alarm signal where one immediately realises that the general public and the media in both India and Europe have been somehow left out from each oters changing identities. They continue to react and interact in the 'old' way and tend to classify each other the way they have done for centuries.

Secondly, it was striking the way the controversy was fanned by the media of both sides. The Indian media went overboard in explaining the crises on racial grounds and the European media also discovered a new hot topic to reopen the age old wounds of racism. These exaggerations, if persisted for a long time, become a part of the system of misinformation between both groups and tend to distort the real image. Lakshmi Mittal, used the media and public opinion to his benefit to make his business ends meet and of course Guy Dolle's crude comments did the rest of the work.

The role of the media in provoking and forming new identities has been much studied in the past. Therefore, in the case of India and Europe, the most powerful means of exchanging new ideas of newly found identities would be the media.

Thirdly, conspicuous by their absence, were lobbying and interest groups. It was Lakshmi Mittal alone here in Europe, fighting for his case and using the Indian government and Indian public opinion to his benefit. If this had been the US, where the Indian diaspora is very politically and culturally active, it probably would have been a smoother ride for the Mittals. There are very few people of Indian origin in the parliaments of member states and there are even fewer interest or pressure groups, facilitating and forwarding Indians' interests. The Indian diaspora in the UK, apart from publishing some articles on their websites and making a few noises, was largely absent from the scene. And in any case the United Kingdom was not directly involved in the conflict.

This conflict points to the lack of organised diasporic links, and calls for the formations of caucus like structures, the likes of which are present in the US Senate. The India-US deal is widely proclaimed as a victory of the Indian Caucus in the Senate. India-European relations will probably increase with the increased participation in politics of people of Indian origin in European countries.

Conclusions

One may have to concede that Arcelor's behaviour was pre-planned and was angled for Mittal to increase his bid, which he did. The difference between the first and the third bid was a difference of $12 Euros. Lakshmi Mittal ceded his family's control over the company and reduced its holding to 43.5 per cent, agreed for Guy Dollé to be the head of the board of directors till September 2007 and also agreed for Arcelor to have four seats in the management board, as opposed to his family's three seats.

Although Arcelor ended up increasing its value threefold, I am convinced Guy Dolle's comments had nothing to do with corporate cleverness or pre meditated intelligence.

In addition, responses of the French, Spanish and Luxembourgian governments and of their trade Unions can be explained by the logic of a fear of job losses. However, true, as it might be to a certain extent, their disproportionate response makes one wonder of their particularly strong rancour against the Mittal Steel Company.

Out of all the parties involved, Mittal appears to have been the most ingenious. He played up the Indians national identities by calling Guy Doll's cynicism racist but finally won because of his truest allies: the shareholders. He made several deals with shareholders, and realised rightly that they are the final key to his success. He promised the Arcelor board of directors that he would step down as chief and agreed to keep Guy Dolle at the helm, but the moment he secured the company, he sacked the entire board and became CEO of the new steel giant.

My concluding remarks would be to wonder if Dubai Ports, on the other side of the Atlantic, faced a similar situation. Although the context is more complex, being mixed with the war on terror, nevertheless, the ramifications on the identity question, may be comparable.

References

Miles, R. (1989). *Racism*. London: Routledge.

Rattansi, A. (1995). *Race, Education, Society: A Study Guide*, Open University, Milton Keynes.

Wetherell, Margaret (1996). "Group Conflict and the Social Psychology of Racism" in Wetherell, Margeret (ed.), *Identites, Groups and Social Issues*. London: Sage Publications. pp.175-238.

8

A Mechanism for Enhancing EU-India Software Development Collaboration

An Institutional Perspective

SUDHANSHU RAI

Introduction

This paper is about forwarding an argument to the merits of developing a inclusive research agenda, including the analysis of culture from a micro-perspective and relying on institutions and institutional logics in particular to develop a richer understanding of the epistemic differences that make cultures diverse. Section 2 roots this analysis in a real world experience. This experience suggests that for firms to learn how software development is perceived in different cultures, a better understanding of institutional logic is necessary. Section 3 discusses the theoretical sensitivity, it begins the analysis with general information system thinking, it then moves into a cultural perspective, finally introducing institutional logic as an appropriate tool for analysing Information System Development (ISD) from a cultural perspective. Section 4 introduces Indian reasoning as an example of institutional logic, Section 5 discusses the outcome and section 6 concludes.

Setting the Context

After placing my laptop on my workstation and turning on the air conditioner, I readied myself for the day's work, the time being 9.30 a.m. in New Delhi at Trust4Health during March 1999. Here, I was directing the development of software for a pioneering insurance health service to be launched in October of 2000, in India. As the computer rebooted three of my colleagues walked in with a glum look on their faces. One was manager-system design, the other was programming and testing head and the third was a business analyst. They initiated their conversation by saying:

Sir, we simply cannot agree,

Puzzled and not aware of the context I asked, "What is the matter?"

The problem it appeared, was about new design methodologies and software coding processes that we had introduced to streamline the software production process. The complaint was that the new object oriented methodologies were not really doing what they were supposed to do, while the methodology was logical and sounded simple on paper, in reality this new way of developing software was posing unimaginable challenges to developers, managers and analysts as my subordinates reported that day.

At that time I could not understand how a logically consistent development method was causing ill feeling amongst the group. I could not understand how the internal dynamics of who did what and when was not being adhered to in practice. I simply could not understand how responsible function heads were not able to drive sense into their subordinate's mind and what made them come to me?

Theoretical Sensitivity

Information System Thinking and Practice

I will discuss the nature of information system development, the meaning of methodology within this paradigm and the accompanying social assumptions, pointing out that information systems have overlooked the role of institutions during conceptualisation, design and development, institutions meaning the beliefs, values, norms and social systems of indigenous groups. Developing systems without understanding the embedded nature of institutional logic during the software development process, has the potential to result in the needs of the clients being misperceived.

Information system in itself is embedded in design science, which in turn draws its rational from engineering science, as argued by the book, *The Science of the Artificial,* (Simon, 1996). The design tradition that has given rise to what we know as information systems has a similar methodological tradition, (Silver, *et al.,* 1995). This tradition preoccupies itself with determining the nature of truth, by employing logically consistent arguments in terms of its singularity. To discover truth, the elements perceptively connected to the truth needs to be sterilised for its impact on other related factors to be understood. Such a method uses decomposition as a primary tool for its investigations.

Problem formulation is then within the perimeters of such assumptions that draw on institutional logic to propose solutions. In this case truth (justified theory) and utility (artefacts that are affective) are two sides of the same coin and that scientific inquiry is evaluated on the nature of its practical contribution, (Aboulafia, 1991). Consequently, the truth and the validity of knowledge is predicated on a philosophy of science that demands logical consistency as its key tenant. Information systems as an academic field employ similar logical tradition for its legitimisation. These logical traditions are the embedded institutional logic.

A methodology relates to an activity that relies on deconstructing the knowledge base and the problem domain; "Deconstruction is the process of disassembling socially constructed meanings that have been coded in texts" (Eisenhardt, 1989). The problem solving focus of design science and early system thinkers assumes that formal systematic approach to developing a solution to societies problems is the most effective way to solve social needs. It is best served by a causality driven systematic approach to design. Relying on a method that supposes the modularisation of the problem appears to be an effective way to control software development, (Klein and Kraft, 1994; Kraft and Truex, 1994). The role of decomposition is to provide a logical approach to reaching an objective (Yourdon and Constantine, 1979). The predetermined objectives, systematic methods, the prescriptive nature of truth all drive institutionalised knowledge, that in its core, consists of a set of institutional logic about the best way to develop systems.

The method in information system design then is advocated to be a structured, disciplined practice dealing with the abstraction of the social world. The information system deals with the combination, collaboration and communication of information in a systematic manner, so as to be able to solve the challenges of the physical and natural world. By adopting a structured approach to system design, one can manage and be able to predict a favourable outcome by perceiving designers as experts. The step by step problem solving can be tackled by people embedded in a strict methodology (Silver, *et al.*, 1995). The key being, to design, one requires domain knowledge, i.e., appropriate knowledge, a market argument to why the artifact is useful in solving a problem, if it is an economic one, and then a clear understanding of who needs it most. Such an argument will have institutional logic embedded in them and rely on their own institutions to work the system.

Therefore information system design aims at refining methodology and clarify objectives for the solution of a problem. ISD draws upon three types of resource, The individuals, their cultural values (Kumar and Bjorn-Andersen, 1990), and their beliefs (Greif, 1994). The technology combining it with a knowledge base and the existence of a supporting physical infrastructure, (Castells, 1996; Ciborra and Hanseth, 1999) suggests an important role of the individual in the process of systems development. This implies that for any artifact to be designed, one needs to have some level of diffusion of appropriate technologies (Feldman and Florida, 1994; Soete, 1984; O'Neill, Pouder, and Buchholtz, 1998). As design results are codified using the knowledge base, system building is then the routine application of the knowledge base to known problems (Hevner, Ram, March, and Park, 2004), and design methodology is adopted by designers at the confluence of technology and people (Lee, 2000). The confluence then is richly dominated by institutional logic, which are institutionalised, meaning rules and those logics that emerge out of experiences.

Summing Up

What the information systems (IS) paradigm fails to take on board is the role of the individual and his institutional embeddedness, the social logics being used to make sense of experience and the role of this social logic in influencing the perception of system development. This aspect of inquiry has been overlooked in favour of more controlled, systematic and sequential methodologies. It could be interesting to make a departure from studying national, regional, or organisational cultures to studying the role of institutional logic in determining how cultures take advantage of diversity.

Cultural Perceptions of Information Systems

In this section, I aim to illustrate how national and organisational analysis of culture has not assisted in answering the key question. What are the key elements that determine the identification of national and organisational culture in the context of information systems development? In concluding this section; I point out that the treatment of culture has overlooked the role of institutions in influencing information system development.

Discussing culture within an Information system paradigm, Walsham (2002) overlooks the role of institutions, although he has subsequently discussed institutions from a structuration perspective The role of institutional logic in his analysis is implicit. One of his insights suggested that Indian culture appeared not to value the use of maps. His argument for such a statement was an observation that even though people in India carried maps they would stop and ask for directions instead of using the map to find their way. (Walsham, 2002). In their observation they did not address why such an approach was adopted by the Indians they observed. Similarly, (Robertson, 1992) and (Appadurai, 1997) suggest that technology is usurped by indigenous cultures and modified to cater to their own needs. The explanation to why cultures reason differently might be embedded in the way their institutional logic are developed and internalised.

The key here is, if cultures are different, then shouldn't we try and study the drivers of their difference, influenced by their epistemology of Knowledge, (Nisbett, 2003). Instead of limiting our understanding of culture, based on research rooted in notions of differences from a western perspective, (Rajkumar and Mani, 2001; Pauleen and Murphy, 2005) and using value to understand the difference for minimising system conflict (Leidner and Kayworth, 2006), shouldn't we re-orient our research, focusing on how to integrate other non western reasoning traditions, particularly in a fast globalising world? The prognosis looks grim, if we rely on past research as an indicator for what is to come. It is with this spirit I add to the voice of (Pauleen and Murphy, 2005) calling for research that helps our understanding of information system development in diversity, using institutional logics.

Summing Up

The new style can come from being inclusive, by taking note of other epistemologies in addition to a western one. In making a case for an inclusive research agenda I will make two assertions, First, I will demonstrate briefly how Indian reasoning, as an example of a non western epistemology can be incorporated into IS thinking. Second, I will argue that such incorporation will address (Pauleen, Evaristo *et al.*, 2006) concerns about IS as a biased field of inquiry, by attempting to broaden the research agenda. Two objectives would then be fulfilled,

1) An inclusive research agenda has the potential to provide a better understanding of IS thinking from an indigenous perspective and not a western interpretation of a non western situation.
2) An inclusive agenda has the potential to help practitioners to understand IS issues from their own context, (Pauleen, Evaristo *et al.*, 2006).

Institutional Logic as an Additional Analytical Tool

The main motivation in proposing an inclusive agenda for information system research is to attempt a shift of emphasis from studying culture, as a standpoint of difference in relation to western styles of thinking. Instead initiate research rooted in epistemic synthesis. I propose institutional theory. Such a perspective will be normatively rooted. Meaning that this research will depart from the understanding of institutions as an entity that structures behaviour, instead focusing on the activities of individuals embedded in society and culture, with values, beliefs, norms, customs, all affecting economic behaviour. Focusing on how institutional logic might influence the design of information systems, and the way institutions affect their delivery, is of interest.

Specifically, I will engage institutional logic and legitimacy as my guiding light. These ideas can be found within broader institutional literature (Epstein, 1984; Thomas, Meyer *et al.*, 1987; King, Gurhaxani *et al.*, 1994; Thornton and Ocasio, 1999). Evoking institutional logic within an information system paradigm assumes that designers developing IS would presuppose and embed their understanding of what the user needs into the service they conceptualise, perhaps shying away from using the full potential of the technology. If this is so, the question why, would be worth addressing.

Institutional logic can be explicated as the development of a framework which enables the decoding of experiences, using a platform or a reasoning tradition that is consistent to the overall context of a given environment, (Rao, Monin, and Durand, 2003). Horn (1983: 1), defines logic as "the underlying assumptions, deeply held, often unexamined, which form a frame-work within which reasoning takes place", subsequently (Fredlend and Alford, 1983) extended Horn's ideas to apply it to institutions, defining institutional logic to be a "higher-order societal institution, such as the family, religion, government, and pro-organizing principles", that affect individuals and groups. Institutional logic provides "guidelines for practical action" (Rao *et al.*, 2003). They encode the criteria of legitimacy by which role identities, strategic behaviours, organisational forms, and relationships between organisations are constructed and sustained (Greenwood and Hinings, 1996).

Institutional logic enables actors to make sense of their ambiguous world by prescribing actions. Action re-enacts institutional logic, making them durable (Suddaby and Greenwood, 2005). In practice institutional logic can be illustrated by referring to a study of Japanese family values. Institutional logic of collective responsibility attributes the collective nature of Japanese management to the Chinese idea "Ie",(Bhappu, 2000). Further (Martinez and Dacin, 1999) attributed the acceptability of transaction cost to institutional logics in explaining firm behaviour, Similarly, (Thornton and Ocasio, 1999) illustrated the use of institutional logic to help managers acquire legitimacy and move up the organisational hierarchy. (Lounsbury, 2002) illustrated how institutional logic was applied to legitimise the use of financial management in financial firms. In past studies, institutional logic has been identified to have a diverse impact. If institutional logic is an important institutional factor, should we not apply such an analysis to how the development of information system development, is perceived in the West and how that is different from Indian epistemology?

A fair understanding of Institutional logic can help in the acceptance of an information system design by allowing users to get persuaded, provided the firm is able to understand the way people represent their arguments locally (Rai, 2007). For Information System Development (ISD) to be successful, the users need to adopt, understand and accept the embedded institutional logic inherent in an information system design. For this to occur the ISD needs to be consistent with their context.

The creation of legitimacy is important because it provides the environment for reuse and then reuse solidifies institutional logic, making it become an instrument for creating shared experience. This potentially enables the legitimisation of a service over time. Could it be that for an information system to be successful the quality and the trust around that quality needs to be legitimised and that legitimacy "re-negotiated" with each new launch of an e-service in different regions of the world? Such a formulation would imply creation and sustenance of home grown skills, different from the ideas of software integrated around COTS (commercial-off-the-shelf software). The justification for these issues might be embedded in the way cultures and their institutions flourish and influence information system design. If Institutional logic matters; then could a case for developing a local ICT industry be eloquently justified? Studying ISD with the help of institutional logic can provide a unique theoretical perspective for detecting factors in determining how one should structure service delivery in various markets.

Indian Reasoning as an Example of Institutional Logics

The term Indian reasoning is employed here in the broadest sense; it encapsulates historical traditions, in terms of culture, its life philosophy, its religious beliefs and the justification for living. Such justifications are formal arguments that are drawn on two kinds of contexts, one the context of development and the other the context of justification. Often what we are always in tune with is the context of justification, while the context of development is empirical and process dependent. Context of justification is more formal, drawing upon formal arguments. Indian tradition presents scientific methodology using slightly different argumentative formulations. For instance, the nature of inference in an Indian context has an intermediary qualifier, denoted as "*AS*". This qualifier is the contextual qualifier linking an argument to empirical evidence witnessed at least once.

For instance; if we state that "Greeks are mortals; Socrates is a Greek; it then follows that Socrates is mortal." Since my conclusion is correct, the argument is correct given the premise. Using a similar formulation, I can claim that all Martians are blue, Socrates is a Martian therefore Socrates is blue. The line of argument is valid and correct but it is not sound. For instance I cannot demonstrate that there is a Martian and that he is blue. Such inferential formulation in an Indian context is not permitted, but when I add a qualifier like "AS" my inferential formulation gets grounded in an observation that is predicated on the identification of the existence of at least one Martian. On the basis of that empirical evidence my argument would hold good.

Another important criterion for a reasoning tradition that has a potential to enrich system thinking is the "Tri-Rupia" or the three conditions, suggested by "Dignavaya" (Matilal, 1998). The "Tri-rupia" or the three inferential rules stipulate that, when an inference is forwarded for it to be valid and sound, it must obey the "Tri-Rupia" rule. The rule being, for every argument, there must be a similar case, a dissimilar case and a context or an empirical observation of that case for it to hold good. For instance, if I want to infer that sound is non eternal because it dissipates like objects, then first I would need to employ the similarity argument and claim that anything produced, for instance a pot, is non-eternal. The dissimilar argument would be space, which is produced and is not non-eternal. Then I would have to provide a context, instance of at least one observation that satisfies the condition of empirical existence or having been witnessed. The "Tri-rupia" is a form or argument that takes both perspectives, applies it for relevance on empirical validity—meaning an observation that provides the context for both the similar and the dissimilar argument. It is this empirical anchoring that adds relevance and rigour to either of the positions.

Combining this formalism with a "mystic holistic" that persists in India, indicates that the character of Indian thought is a mixture of formal rules rapped around with experiential knowledge. Let me speculate a bit to the engine driving this holism. The key to the holism I surmise is the flexible identity demonstrated by individuals across functional areas. For instance, it is often remarked that scientists and managers in India are as much interested in astrology as science; they are as much at home in the temples and among their customs as they are in research labs or meetings, (Sarukkai, 2005). They are as much at home in front of their parents submitting to their wishes as they are in office submitting to their projects.

Such flexibility and fluidity indicates anecdotally, that culture has an important role to play in the way reasoning is applied. The tri-rupia rule, the qualifier "AS"and the mystic holistic are all types of institutional logic. Some of these logics are formal abstractions of knowledge, others are based on reasoning. For instance, the ability of software developers in an Indian context, given a basket of problems, to arrive at an answer by zooming in on the likely area of the solution on an instinct, without employing elaborate analytical tools suggests a spatial awareness of interconnections, (Rai, 2007). Thus, if the context evolves the potential solution, the problem will also evolve implying the fluidity of the holistic interconnectivity.

Result, A Framework

Information system thinking subscribes to how systems take shape. For those that believe in such a view, the path to discovering the truth is via the systematic application of analytical tenants of decomposition, segregation and modularisation, which aim at determining a problem by identifying the explanatory variable, focusing on its character and relationships with other variables and then working out a solution aiming at integrating it into the system, while others are held constant. Here one deals with clean models, definitive actors, predictable propositions and above all falsifiable theories. We can call this "Representative ability", RA. RA represents aspects of institutional logic that are formalised. They are rules, represented by formal definitions and relationships, laws about nature. Truths about experience and simple rules governing causality influenced by the logic of appropriateness and shared legitimacy. Norms that get enacted under the sphere of influence of RA aim at instilling in actors a standard behaviour or a predictable way of doing things. To achieve the standardisation of action RA draws on facts, figures and general knowledge. All of them work together to institutionalise the individual with institutional logics predicated on RA (Rai, 2007).

In a fast globalising world, with pervasive information technology, where multiple logic exists, cultures abound and reasoning is not subjected to a strict academic tradition. As indigenous people take part in applying Information system thinking to their own lives, in so doing they will naturally push the boundaries by internalising the technology from their own standpoint. Potentially they will reconfigure assumptions, and truths for their own purposes (Robertson, 1992; Appadurai, 1997). The consequence of the pervasive quality of the information system, will inevitably enable the emergence of a inclusive global IS thinking, where all interlocutors will contribute from their own standpoints, thus making the IS field able, to observe other reasoning styles (Pauleen, Evaristo *et al.*, 2006).

Consequently, Indian reasoning is as useful as any indigenous tradition in contributing and learning from information system thinking. Here the reliance is less on formalised knowledge, and rules but institutionalised logic that is experimentally developed. An experiential approach to knowledge is referred to as PC, "Persuasive capacity", (Rai, 2007). PC, which relies on three normative indicators: shared meaning, interactional scripts and cultural markers. These three normative drivers collectively influence norm enactment that depends on the existence of a collegial working environment, a cultural anchor to argumentation and a social frame assisting discourse.

Consequently, shared meaning, interactional scripts and cultural markers[1] affect norm enactment, such that the primary characteristics of these norms are their ability to influence a collective, using the strengths of discourse, reflection and the understanding of an experience for coping with dynamic changes.[2] What is emerging is a

1. Cultural markers have two terms, culture, which I consider as a collection of beliefs and ways of interacting and perceiving experiences and markers, which I see as indicators of identifying one culture. On combination, cultural markers are those beliefs that are synonymous to a particular society.

2. During a discourse the primary dynamic is discussing and the decoding of an experience, the experience can be decoded with a particular structure but it can also be decoded outside a structure. For instance, my travels abroad cannot be understood within the structures of the society I belong to but can be understood through a dialogue with others from that society. This dialogue provides a number of options that I may be able to internalise. The choice of what norm I internalise will depend on how acceptable the explanation of the individual is. It will not depend on the number of facts he uses to convince me but rather the reasons he employs to make me understand an experience. Similarly, norm enactments dominated by the PC are norms emerging out of reason.

dual perspective, one driven by rules and formalised by laws of nature embedded in RA and the other culturally specific, reasoning based embedded in the ability to persuade and encapsulated by the term PC. Both these constructs have their own institutional logic that predicts the nature of the truth, suggests the way to solve problems and are neither strong enough to suppress the other. With increasing globalisation there is likely to be an increase in tension between RA and PC. Tension here should not be construed as negative phenomena but a positive one, (Rai, 2007).

The Tension Model

The tension model is based on a dual view of action and internalised experiences. This means individuals in a team shift their opinions, ideas and beliefs about a locus based on the nature of discourse and the level of opposition. Second, the tension model takes conflict as a normal state of affairs or as given. Hence the proposition of the tension model is not to seek management solutions that avoid

Figure 8.1

The Tension Model

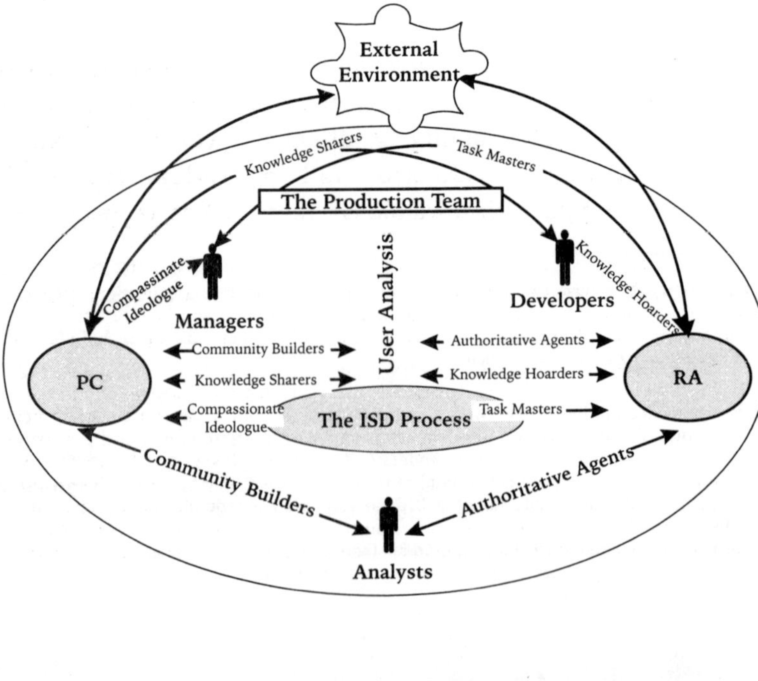

conflict, but to assume conflict as given and inevitable in any interaction inherent to human discourse. It sees conflict as a consequence of weak tension. The tension model suggests a converse relationship between tension and conflict. Implying, enacted norms with diverse positions keep the discourse suspended in a tension, see figure below for an illustration.

Business Benefits from an Inclusive Agenda

I discuss two insights for businesses in this paper. First, businesses that rely on information technology need to be aware of the existence of a system of thinking other than the western dominated procedures and system development processes. In short they should be willing to understand and see the world using institutional logics not their own. Indian reasoning here has been used as an illustration to suggest a difference of institutional logics that might be embedded in cultures. It is most likely that indigenously developed cultures would have their own systems of reasoning giving identity to their value systems making a culture distinct from others, (Kumar and Bjorn-Andersen, 1990; Leidner and Kayworth, 2006). Implications of such an articulation could be manifold, for instance contract writing, leasing agreements, employment practice etc.

Second, incorporating local thinking into their ways of working, they demonstrate respect of the host culture but also lower the cost of training, as new employees don't have to unlearn what they learned, instead build on their own knowledge about the system development that uses the indigenous reasoning style. The firm can develop them and in so doing creates a unique work force that is easier to work with and cheaper to manage. Hence business can ensure sustainability—meaning, the business is able to be sustained in an industry that sees high turnover by incorporating the local perspective on systems design. In doing so employees need not institutionalise in line with western modes of system thinking, instead encouraging locals to reason in a manner that would be similar and consistent with western development methodologies. The main point being, that if indigenously developed, reasoning systems are part of IS, then the potential for misunderstandings or an expensive training programme would be negligible, next to none and at the same time enrich the IS field by incorporating newer ideas leading to innovation in system development methodologies.

Conclusion

The main theme of this paper was to argue for an inclusive IS research agenda bringing into focus institutional analysis, discussing the notion of a valid reasoning tradition based on the role of institutions. Indian reasoning was used to provide an illustration of an example of institutional logic. Such an example fulfilled two purposes; first, it pointed out that other cultures have rich traditions of formal thinking that may be of use in information systems. Second, that institutional logic embedded in western institutions have to work with institutions embedded in non-western reasoning. The tension model was introduced to suggest how such institutional logic might be able to interact.

Coming back to the context, I was not able to understand the predicament of my subordinates as my position institutionalised a set of logics that subscribed to reasoning embedded in the logic of authority. Were I to experience the same situation today, I would probably react differently. For starters, I would explore a bit more on the narratives of subordinates making the complaint, discussing the observation from different angles. This exercise would allow me to acknowledge diversity within the team and use it to enrich the team. I would use tension between diverse interpretations as a tool for a richer interpretation of the situation. By incorporating diverse thinking traditions, richer knowledge can be brought to bear on the problem than the business methodologies currently being adopted.

In summary this paper tries to make four points,

First, it tries to point out that information research has overlooked institutional analysis, in particular the role of institutional logic in system development, an oversight that might limit the insight from cultural analysis of information systems

Second, institutional logic provides the tools for decoding factual as well as divergent experiences.

Third, institutional logic may provide a better chance for dealing with challenges facing distributed work across diverse cultural and geographical regions.

Fourthly, a serious concerted effort needs to be made in trying to incorporate indigenous systems of thinking into information system methodologies, doing so will make information system thinking and the IS field truly global. Attempts made (Pauleen, Evaristo *et al.*, 2006) in drawing our attention to our bias, favouring one type of research and calling it global is a welcome effort. I attempt to strengthen their argument by making concrete suggestions in pointing out that the consideration of institutional logic as an analytical framework ought to explain the difference and help organisations to synthesise and work with diverse cultures.

References

Aboulafia, M. (1991). *Philosophy, Social Theory, and the Thought of George Herbert [2] Mead.* New York: State University of New York Press.

Appadurai, A. (1997). *Modernity at Large: Cultural Dimension sof Globalization.* New Delhi, India: Oxford University Press.

Bhappu, A.D. (2000). "The Japanese Family: An Institutional Logic for Japanese Corporate Networks and Japanese Management", *Academy of Management Review* **25**(2).

Castells, M. (2000). "Materials for an Explanatory Theory of Network Society", *British Journal of Sociology* 51(1): 5-24.

———. (1996). *The Rise of the Network Society.* Massachusetts: Blackwell Publishers Inc.

Ciborra, C.U. and O. Hanseth (1999). *From Control to Drift.* Oxford: Oxford University Press.

Epstein, E. C. (1984). "Legitimacy, Institutionalization, and Opposition in Exclusionary Bureaucratic-Authoritarian Regimes: The Situation of the 1980s", *Comparative Politics* **17**(1): 37-54.

Feldman, M.P. and R. Florida (1994). "The Geographic Sources of Innovation: Technological Infrastructure and Product Innovation in the United States", *Annals of the Association of American Geographers* 84(2): 210.

Greenwood, R. and C.R. Hinings (1988). "Organizational Design Types, Tracks and the Dynamics of Strategic Change", *Organization Studies* 9(3): 293-316.

Greif, A. (1994). "Cultural Beliefs and the Organization of Society: A Historical and Theoretical Reflection on Collectivist and Individualist Societies", *The Journal of Political Economy* 102(5): 912-950.

Hevner, Alan R., Sudha Ram *et al.* (2004). "Design Science and Information Systems Research", *MIS Quarterly* 28(1): 75-10.

King, J.L., V. Gurhaxani *et al.* (1994). "Institutional Factors in Information Technology Innovation", *Information Systems Research* **5**(2).

Klein H.K. and P. Kraft (1994). "Social Control and Social Contract in Networking", *Computer Supported Cooperative Work* 2: 89-108.

Kraft, P. and D. Truex (1994). "Postmodern Management and Information Technology in the Modern Industrial Corporation", in R. Baskerville and S. Smithson (eds.), *Information Technology and New Emergent Forms of Organizations.* Amsterdam: Elsevier Science. pp.113-127.

Kumar, K. and N. Bjorn-Andersen (1990). "A Cross-cultural Comparison of IS Designer Values", *Communications of the ACM* **33**(5).

Lee, A. (2000). "Systems Thinking, Design Science, and Paradigms: Heeding Three Lessons from the Past to Resolve Three Dilemmas in the Present to Direct a Trajectory for Future Research in the Information Systems Field", Keynote Address. *Eleventh International Conference on Information Management*. Taiwan.

Leidner, D.E. and T. Kayworth (2006). "A Review of Culture in Information Systems Research: Towards a Theory of Information Technology Culture Conflict", *MIS Quarterly* **30**(2).

Martinez, R.J. and T.M. Dacin (1999). "Efficiency Motives and Normative Force, Combining Transactions Costs and institutionai Logic", *Journal of Management* **25**(1): 75-96.

Matilal, B.K. (1998). *The Character of Logic in India*. New York: State University of New York.

Meyer, J.W., J. Boli *et al.* (1987). "Ontology and Rationalization in the Western Cultural Account: Nouvelle Cuisine as an Identity Movement in French Gastronomy", *American Journal of Sociology* 108(4).

Nisbett, R. (2003). *The Geography of Thought, How Asians and Westerners Think Differently...and Why*. New York: The Free Press.

O'Neill, Hugh M., Richard W. Pouder *et al.* (1998). "Patterns in the Diffusion of Strategies across Organizations: Insights from the Innovation Diffusion Literature", *Academy of Management Review* 23(1): 98-114.

Pauleen, D.J. and P. Murphy (2005). "In Praise of Cultural Bias", *MIT Sloan Management Review* **46**(2).

Pauleen, D.J., R. Evaristo *et al.* (2006). "Cultural Bias in Information Systems Research and Practice: Are You Coming from the Same place I Am?", *Communication of the Association for Information System* 17: 364-372.

Rai, S. (2007). *Where Process is the Objective; Exploring the Relationship between Analysts, Developers and Managers in an IT project in India: An Institutionalization Perspective*, Published PhD. Copenhagen: Copenhagen Business School. pp.350.

Rajkumar, T.M. and R.V.S. Mani (2001). *Outsourcing Offshore Software Development*.

Rao, Hayagreeva, Monin Philippe *et al.* (2003). "Institutional Change in Toque Ville:

Robertson, R. (1992). *Globalization: Social Theory and Global Culture*.

Roger Fredlend and Robert R. Alford (1983). "Bringing Society Back", Walter W. Powel and Paul J. DiMaggio (eds.), *Symbols, Practices, and Institutional Contradictions. The New Institutionalism in Organisational Theory*. Chicago and London: Chicago University Press.

Sarukkai, S. (2005). *Indian Philosophy and the Philosophy of Science*. New Delhi: Motilal Banarsidass Publishers (P) Limited.

Silver, M.S., M.L. Markus *et al.* (1995). "The Information Technology Interaction Model: A Foundation for the MBA Core Course", *MIS Quarterly* 19(3): 361-390.

Simon, H.A. (1996). *The Sciences of the Artificial*. Cambridge, MA, MIT Press.

Suddaby, R. and R. Greenwood (2005). "Rhetorical Strategies of Legitimacy", Administrative Science Quarterly 50: 35-67.

Thomas, M., J.W. Meyer *et al.* (eds.) (1987). *Institutional Structure: Constituting State, Society, and the Individual*. Newbury Park, CA: Sage.

Thornton, P.H. and W. Ocasio (1999). "Institutional Logics and the Historical Contingency of Power in Organizations: Executive Succession in the Higher Education Publishing Industry, 1958-1991", *American Journal of Sociology* **105**(3): 801-43.

Walsham, G. (2002). "Cross-Cultural Software Production and Use: A Structurational Analysis", *MIS Quarterty* **26**(4): 359-380.

Yourdon, E. and L. Constantine (1979). *Structured Design*. Englewood Cliffs, NJ, USA: Prentice-Hall.

9

Prospects and Challenges of EU-India Security Cooperation

ANNEGRET BENDIEK and CHRISTIAN WAGNER

Introduction

The European Union (EU) and India have intensified their relations since the mid 1990s. With the first bilateral summit in Lisbon 2000, the EU acknowledged that India is going to play a more important role in the international system in the 21st century. The strategic partnership agreement of 2004, the joint action plan of 2005, and the country strategy paper for EU-India relations until 2013 have further broadened their relationship from economic relations to political and strategic issues. A closer look reveals also that India—EU relations are still characterised by traditional forms of cooperation in which security matters are only of secondary importance. During her visit to India in February 2007, European Commissioner for External Relations and European Neighbourhood Policy, Benita Ferrero Waldner, announced that the European Commission is proposing substantial financial assistance to India over the next seven years. An amount of 470 million Euros should be available between 2007-2013. But 60 to 70 per cent of the funds will be used for social sector support especially health and education, to achieve India's Millennium Development Goals (MDG). Thirty to 40 per cent will be used for the implementation of the joint action plan but even here the focus is on economic sectoral dialogues, culture, civil society and academic exchange.[1] The financial distribution seems to indicate that security cooperation will be limited more to ministerial meetings and regular exchanges rather than on joint international initiatives or common activities for regional conflict resolution. However, the EU and India

1. *India, Country Strategy Paper 2007–2013*, p.16.

have both identified security as one pillar of their future cooperation. Future security cooperation is deeply rooted in their different historical foreign policy traditions and therefore limited not only because of the intergovernmental nature of foreign and security policy within the EU. To evaluate the prospects and challenges of security cooperation the paper will first analyse the principles and objectives of security as they are laid out in official documents. Secondly, an analysis of two areas of common concern i.e. regional conflicts/failed states, and non-proliferation and multilateralism reveals parallel rather than joined strategies.

Principles and Objectives for Security Cooperation

Security cooperation between India and the EU was strongly influenced by the terrorist attacks of September 11th in the United States (US). In reaction to these events the National Security Strategy of 2002 proclaimed the "Global War on Terror" (GWoT). On the basis of freedom and democracy the U.S. wanted to struggle against so called "rogue states", global terror networks and trans-national terrorist groups, such as Al Qaeda[2] with the support of like-minded states. However, the US "war on terror" reflected a traditional external policy response to a security threat in the sense that it sought to solve problems by military intervention.

In contrast to this, terrorist attacks in Europe like the bombings in Madrid of March 11th, 2004 and in London in July 2005 initiated a so-called 'securitisation' of European agendas by bridging the gap between internal and external security matters. The Europeans' concern for reinforcing their multidimensional and multilateral vision of regional and international security was set out by the European Security Strategy (ESS).[3] Adopted on 12 December 2003 by the European Council, the ESS highlighted the future importance of the EU in restructuring security in Europe and became one of the main documents in the EU's security strategy policy.[4] For the very first

2. *National Security Strategy of the United States of America*. Washington D.C.: White House. September 2002.

3. *A Secure Europe in a Better World: European Security Strategy*. Brussels: European Council. December 1, 2003. *http://ue.eu.int/uedocs/cmsUpload/78367.10-01-06*

4. Ibid.

time, the EU explicitly identified key threats to its security and the lines of defence. The selection of these threats was based on the use of the multidimensional concept of security; hence poverty, pandemics and competition for natural or energy resources were incorporated alongside terrorism, international organized crime, the proliferation of weapons of mass destruction and regional conflicts such as *inter alia* in the Middle East.

Figure 9.1

Threats According to the European Security Strategy

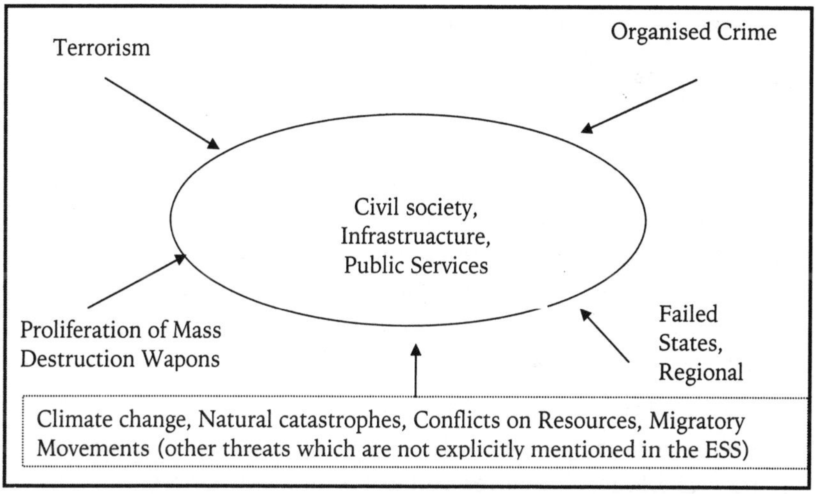

The ESS highlights that the EU must develop the capacity to send missions to distant places and contribute to international security by exercising effective multilateralism, international co-operation and the strengthening of multilateral institutions. It states that active engagement is also in the EU's security interest, since it is negatively affected by poor governance, insecurity, poverty and conflicts far beyond its borders. However, it excludes the military option in the sense of pre-emptive strikes as stated in the National Security Strategy of the United States. According to the ESS, the EU has therefore three key foreign policy objectives in developing its foreign policy tool box to meet contemporary security challenges:[5]

5. *European Security Strategy*. pp.7-14.

a. extending the security zone on Europe's periphery,
b. supporting the emergence of a stable and equitable international order, particularly an effective multilateral system, and
c. seeking effective countermeasures to new and old threats.

Beyond the efforts to extend Europe's security zone on its periphery, the EU is highly engaged in promoting its model of integration in other parts of the world. While the European Union as a supranational organisation *sui generis* cannot claim the same degree of power and influence as the United States in the international system, it has an increasing degree of influence through its so-called soft power. European strategy does not only go hand in hand with the idea of selling the concept of the European model of regional integration; it also insists on a commitment to strong multilateral institutions.

The EU strategy of building so-called strategic partnerships beyond the US and Russia with new emerging powers such as China, Japan, Brazil, Canada and India was very much triggered by the launching of the ESS. The Common Foreign and Security Policy (CSFP) capacity building in respect to new emerging powers must be seen in a broader international context, rather than in the narrower EU/European context.[6]

The situation in India differs both from the US and the EU. Since a number of years, terrorism has been regarded as the main domestic security challenge, however India has not yet formulated a concise national security strategy. Nevertheless the main pillars of India's security strategy can be extracted out of speeches given by the prime minister, and the minister of external affairs and documents from the ministry of defence.[7] India and Europe have common security concerns in preventing states from failing and in the fight against terrorism.

6. Sjursen, Helene (2006). "What Kind of Power?", in *Journal of European Public Policy* 13(2): S.235-51, March; Rosamond, Ben (2005). "Conceptualizing the EU Model of Governance in World Politics", in *European Foreign Affairs Review* 10 (4): S. 463-478, Winter ; Thym, Daniel, Weiche (2005). "Konstitutionalisierung–Optionen der Umsetzung einzelner Reformschritte des Verfassungsvertrags ohne Vertragsänderung", in *Integration* 28 (5): S.307-15, Oktober.

7. Extracts of PM's address at the Combined Commander's Conference, New Delhi 18.10.06, in *http://pmindia.nic.in/lspeech.asp?id=432* (accessed 20.10.06); Address by the External Affairs Minister on the occasion of the National launch of Global India Foundation, *India and the Global Balance of Power*, 16/01/2007, in *http://meaindia.nic.in/speech/2007/01/16ss02.htm* (accessed 18.1.07); Ministry of Defence. *Annual Report Year 2005-006*, in *http://mod.nic.in/reports/welcome.html* (accessed 9.3.07).

Prime Minister Manmohan Singh has stated that India "cannot afford to see states fail." Moreover, both Europe and India share new security threats that are related to poverty, pandemics and organised crime. The EU put, furthermore, a focus on topics such as "conflict prevention and post-conflict reconstruction", "Democracy and human rights" and "Peace, Prosperity and stability in South Asia."[8] India's foreign minister stated in January 2007 that his country is not interested in "exporting ideology" which underlined again the different approach.[9]

Historically, bilateral relations can be traced back to the 1960s. But it was only in the 1990s that India received greater attention in the EU because of her economic success after liberalisation in 1991. The first summit in Lisbon in 2000 can be considered as a preparatory meeting for establishing the strategic partnership which brought India in the same line with countries like the US, China, Russia, Japan, and Canada which with the EU also held regular summit meetings. Issues dealt within bilateral relations such as EU-India relations range across different matters. These different relations include bilateral trade issues, sectoral policy issues, competition matters, transport policy cooperation, visa issues, the fight against terrorism etc. Particular progress was made at the Hague Summit in November 2004, culminating in the approval of a plan mapping out the so-called 'strategic partnership' in the course of the summit under the British EU-presidency. In September 2005, the EU and India adopted an ambitious and wide-ranging 'joint action plan' which set the course for future EU-India strategic partnership. In the Joint Action Plan of September 2005 both sides agreed among other things on a number of exchanges, consultative mechanisms and dialogues on various political levels on "Democracy and Human Rights", "Effective Multilateralism", "Peacekeeping, Peace-Building and Post-Conflict Assistance", "Disarmament and Non-Proliferation of WMD and Security Dialogue."[10] The consensus on security issues was followed

8. Commission of the European Communities, Communication from the Commission to the Council, the European Parliament and the European Economic and Social Committee, An EU-India Strategic Partnership, Brussels, June, 16th, 2006.
9. Varadarajan, Siddharth (2007). "India not interested in exporting ideology: Pranab", in *The Hindu*. January 20.
10. Council of the European Union (2005) *The India-EU Strategic Partnership Joint Action Plan*. Brussels. September 07.

by closer collaboration for instance in the field of terrorism.[11] It was the terrorist attacks in New York and Washington and those in Europe that triggered the EU, and again under the British presidency in 2005, to define counter-terrorism as a threat to its security. A joint EU-India working group has been established on counter-terrorism and the issue has been on the agenda at senior officials, ministerial and summit meetings. The EU has imposed a ban on terrorist organisations on its territory—which includes organisations of concern to India—and has also given support to Indian initiatives such as the draft Comprehensive Convention on Terrorism at the UN. Contacts between Indian and EU counter-terrorism coordinators have been established. The EU Counter-Terrorism Coordinator visited New Delhi in October 2006 to establish contact with his Indian Counterpart.[12]

In contrast to Europe, militant Islamic fundamentalism is not a new phenomenon in India. Since the late 1980s Islamist groups have been fighting in Kashmir for accession to Pakistan. The support of these groups from Pakistan triggered various bilateral crisis in the 1990s. The attack on the Indian parliament in December 2001 led to another deep crisis between both countries in summer 2002. With the bilateral rapprochement in 2003–04 infiltration in Kashmir came down but various incidents in Delhi, Mumbai and on the "peace train" in 2007 are related to militant Islamist groups wanting to undermine the peace process. Besides this, India is confronted with a variety of ethnic rebellions like in the northeast and militant communist groups (Naxalites), that operate in various states. The different terrorist movements need a specific approach. India has intensified the political process with Pakistan and Kashmiri groups to find a political solution to the Kashmir issue. After the bombings in Mumbai, in 2006, India and Pakistan agreed to set up a joint mechanism to cooperate against terrorist activities. The Indian government is also engaged in political negotiations with militant groups in the northeast. At the same time it has intensified bilateral relations with neighbouring countries like Bangladesh, Bhutan and Myanmar to fight terrorism. The most

11. European Commission (2007). *The European Union and India: A Strategic Partnership for the 21st Century*. Brussels. *http://es.europa.eu/comm/external_relations/I, 29.3.07*

12. *EU-India Joint Action Plan: Implementation Report*. EU-India Summit. Helsinki, October 13 , 2006. *http://ec.europa.eu/comm/external_relations/india, 293.07*

difficult challenge are the activities of the Naxalites in the rural hinterland of India. All attempts by state governments have not yet brought a political solution.

Despite broad commonalities two challenges stand out in which India and the EU have different foreign policy approaches. One is the complex of failed states and regional conflicts, the other is non-proliferation of weapons of mass destruction and the concept of multilateralism.

Challenges for Security Cooperation

Failed States/Regional Conflicts

Failed states have developed into one of the most important security challenges since the attacks of September 11th, 2001. While India has a long experience of supporting the efforts of the international community to prevent state failure by UN-missions, the question is more difficult to solve for India in her immediate neighbourhood. But in contrast to Europe which is willing to promote good governance and democracy, India pursues a policy of not promoting any ideology based on international norms and values *vis-a-vis* third countries.[13] Looking at the different experiences of India and Europe in dealing with states failure and regional conflicts demonstrate the possibilities and limitations of security cooperation.

Sri Lanka

Although India has a long standing tradition of supporting the efforts of the international community to prevent state failure with the help of UN peace keeping missions, Indian governments have preferred a bilateral approach to deal with security problems in the immediate neighbourhood. During the 1970s and 1980s India regarded South Asia as part of her national security and tried to interfere in neighbouring countries in order to pursue her interests.[14] India's most ambitious attempt for regional conflict resolution was the deployment

13. Ministry of Defence. *Annual Report 2005-06*. New-Delhi. p.12.
14. Wagner, Christian (2005). "From Hard Power to Soft Power? Ideas, Interaction, Institutions, and Images in India's South Asia Policy" *Heidelberg Papers in South Asian and Comparative Politics*. Working Paper No. 26.

of Indian Peace Keeping Forces (IPKF) in Sri Lanka from 1987 to 1990. It was the only Indian military deployment based on a bilateral agreement with the Sri Lankan government and the separatist Liberation Tigers of Tamil Eelam (LTTE) but without the mandate of the UN. The IPKF mission became a political and military fiasco. Shortly after deployment, the IPKF became involved in military confrontation with the LTTE. Because of another militant uprising in the southern part of the country by radical Sinhalese nationalist groups which feared the IPKF would control the whole country, the Sri Lankan government had to withdrew from previous arrangements with India. In the spring of 1990, the last IPKF troops left Sri Lanka.[15] After negative experiences in the 1970s and 1980s Indian governments have been pursuing a different approach since the 1990s. Instead of political interference they emphasised bi- and multilateral economic collaboration with neighbours. This led to the SAARC Preferential Trading Arrangement (SAPTA) in 1995, that developed into the SAARC Free Trade Area (SAFTA) in 2006 and the Free Trade Agreement with Sri Lanka in 1998. India's new neighbourhood policy which stressed the need for non-reciprocity in India's relations with her neighbours was first formulated by Prime minister Gujral in the mid-1990s. In contrast to Europe, India is reluctant to promote actively good governance and democracy in neighbouring countries but supported mediation efforts by outside powers in regional conflicts, a strategy that would have been unthinkable in the 1980s. This new strategy has opened the way for Norway's mediation efforts in Sri Lanka since 2000. Although India is closely incorporated in the process of mediation, it has refused to become a formal member of the Co-Chairs. Since 2003 the EU is one of the Co-Chairs besides Norway, the United States and Japan in the peace process. With the Tokyo conference on reconstruction and development in Sri Lanka, in June 2003, the international community provided massive financial support to facilitate the peace process after the ceasefire agreement (CFA) between the Sri Lankan government and the separatist Liberation Tigers of Tamil Eelam (LTTE) in February 2002. The donor community sent a strong message of political support and provided pledges of US$

15. Muni, S.D. (1993). *Pangs of Proximity. India and Sri Lanka's Ethnic Crisis.* New Delhi.

4.5 billion (grants and loans), tied to progress in the peace process. The conference agreed that the four Co-Chairs would continue to meet regularly and monitor progress in the peace process. The group met four times in 2005, including twice in Brussels (25 January and 19 December). In the context of the Co-Chair group, the EU is represented by the Presidency and the Commission. The EU has played a constructive part as a Co-Chair, providing support to the peace process and to Norway's role as facilitator. Besides financial commitments the Nordic member states of the EU were also engaged in the Sri Lanka Monitoring Mission (SLMM) that was set up to supervise the ceasefire agreement in collaboration with Norway and Iceland. The limitations of the EU engagement became obvious in 2006, when the EU decided to list the LTTE as a terrorist group in Europe, in order to sanction violations of the CFA. In reaction to this the LTTE requested EU members of the SLMM to leave the country so that the SLMM became de facto defunct.

Nepal

The second conflict where India and the EU meet in South Asia is in Nepal, where a militant Maoist movement has challenged the monarchy and political parties since 1996. Because of the open border between both countries, Nepali Maoists received support from Maoist groups operating in India. Nepal is an interesting case because India, for the first time since 1991, has decided to intervene politically in the conflict. The peace agreements of 2006 in Nepal between the Maoist movement and the seven party alliance were arranged with the help of India. Some of the negotiations between both sides took place in India with the open or secret benevolence of the Indian government. With the establishment of a UN mission in Nepal, India and the EU will intensify their efforts to start the process of a constitutional assembly that will be elected in 2007. The first European Commission Country Strategy Paper for Nepal covers the period 2002–2006. The cooperation strategy identifies three major areas for intervention: Long-term support for poverty reduction and interventions in the rural sector, focus on the Mid-Western Regions and the development of renewable energy (photovoltaic) for remote areas with no access to electricity (€ 56 million). Strong emphasis is given to a Preventive Conflict Mitigation

Strategy, supporting conflict mitigation and consolidation of democracy through the judicial sector and promotion of human rights (€10 million). The most immediate objective of this strategy is to reduce social unrest, to promote necessary reforms and to strengthen the role of civil society. India is the most important bilateral trading partner and has also intensified her economic relations in order to assist the reconstruction of the country.[16] Nepal will be an interesting case to see how far India and the EU will be able to strengthen their bilateral relations in regard to conflict mediation in the coming years.

Afghanistan

Finally, failed states and lack of governance may provide areas of retreat for trans-national terrorist groups like Al-Qaida in Afghanistan. Both India and the EU also support international reconstruction efforts in Afghanistan. India is not part of the Western alliance but has increased her economic cooperation with the Afghan government. In 2002, India announced 100 Million US-Dollars in financial assistance for Afghanistan and offered food and humanitarian assistance. In the field of security, India is engaged in the training of police officers and reconstruction of roads by the Border Roads Organisation (BRO). The stationing of paramilitary personnel for the protection of Indian workers against attacks by the Taliban and the planned training of the Afghanistan National Army will further increase India's engagement. In November 2005, the EU and Afghanistan adopted a Joint Declaration setting out a new partnership. The Joint Declaration outlines increased co-operation, based on Afghan ownership, across a range of areas. These include support to political and economic governance; security sector and justice sector reform; counter-narcotics; development; human rights, civil society and refugee return; education and culture. It also establishes a regular political dialogue, with annual meetings at the Ministerial level, and reaffirmed the EU's long-term commitment to Afghanistan as the Bonn process drew to a close. In January 2006, just ahead of the London conference, the Council adopted conclusions welcoming the launch of the Afghanistan Compact on the basis of partnership between the Afghan Government,

---

16. Roy, Bhaskar (2006). "Himalayan Marshall Plan to Bail Out Nepal?", in *Times of India*, April 27.

with its sovereign responsibilities, and the international community, with a central and impartial coordinating role for the United Nations. The Council reaffirmed the EU's support for key pillars of activity identified by the Compact, its commitment to long-term support for the Government and people of Afghanistan through Afghan-led reconstruction efforts and its wish to further enhance the effectiveness of its action. The European Commission has adopted an €18 million humanitarian aid decision to assist the most vulnerable people affected by armed conflict and natural disasters in the regions of Afghanistan, Iran and Pakistan. This funding will benefit returning refugees, internally displaced persons (IDPs) and their host communities. Relief will be provided in the form of shelter and basic services, such as water and sanitation. All funds will be channelled through the European Commission Humanitarian Aid department (ECHO). The EU is furthermore preparing a rule of law mission for Afghanistan in the context of the CFSP/ESDP. Last but not the least, single EU member states, implicitly confirm what had already become a reality through the war in Afghanistan: namely that military means can be used to combat terrorism in third states.

Traditionally, the EU has so far focused its security efforts in its immediate neighbourhood, especially since the collapse of communism in Eastern Europe, in the early 1990s. Interventions in Asia to support the reconstruction of failed states were mainly limited to various EU Election Observer missions. Nevertheless their reports about free and fair elections became important instruments in the negotiations of the EU with respective governments. The EU Monitoring Mission in Aceh (AMM) Indonesia, marks a new step on the path of the EU in becoming a global player. The authoritative mediation through Maarti Ahtisaari, contributed much to bringing the negotiations to a peaceful outcome in July 2005. The EU proved willing and able to take over from there and launch a mission to monitor the peace agreement in the space of a few weeks. The ESDP mission has been judged as a successful and effective contribution in ending years of fighting and paving the way for sustainable peace: "The added value of the European intervention consists in the effective coordination of EU tools to both reconstruct the region ravaged by the tsunami and sustain the political process of reconciliation by facilitating reintegration and consolidating local administration. Coordination matters not only between EU actors but also with international partners. The AMM includes the sizeable contribution of five member countries of the Association of Southeast Asian Nations (ASEAN). This is tangible evidence of the EU's commitment to promoting regional organisations as pillar of effective multilateralism."[17]

Non-proliferation and Multilateralism

In parallel to the launching of the ESS, in December 2003, the EU adopted a Strategy against the proliferation of WMD which state that WMD and missile proliferation put at risk the security of EU Member States. The EU must act with resolve, using all instruments and policies at its disposal. The ultimate objective is to prevent, deter, halt and where possible, eliminate WMD proliferation programmes of concern worldwide. India and the EU seem, however, to have opposing positions in the field of proliferation. The EU and all its member states have been strong proponents of the Non-Proliferation Treaty (NPT) since the beginning. Although Indian governments have always propagated global nuclear disarmament they have refused to enter the NPT. With the first nuclear test in 1974, India isolated herself and was confronted with a series of sanctions. After the second series of tests in 1998, India faced again strong international criticism and sanctions but the Indian government underlined that it is willing to abide by the main principles of the NPT even if it will not sign it. Despite their divergent views, India and the EU were able to narrow down their differences in the strategic partnership agreement of 2004. A compromise could be found in emphasising common efforts to prevent the proliferation of weapons of mass destruction (WMD) thereby renouncing any reference to India's own nuclear ambitions. India's good record in the field of non-proliferation was acknowledged with the agreement on civilian nuclear cooperation with the United States in March 2006. The agreement initiated a debate on how far this would strengthen or weaken the NPT. It also created a problem for the EU because member countries were split in their reaction. In reaction

17. Brau, Pierre-Antoine and Grevi, Giovanni (2005). "The EU Mission in Aceh: Implementing Peace", *Occasional Paper* No. 61. December. Paris: European Union Institute for Security Studies. S.1-37(3).

to the Indo-US nuclear deal, the EU announced, in February 2007, that India should take a 'few steps' like associating with the NPT and Comprehensive Test Ban Treaty (CTBT) before it can decide on cooperating with it in civil nuclear energy. The EU is expecting India will take steps towards an international non-proliferation mechanism, and then swiftly conclude safeguard agreements with the International Atomic Energy Agency (IAEA). The EU is reflecting the continuing ambivalence among Europeans countries towards civilian nuclear energy cooperation with India. Britain and France have come out strongly in support of the India-US nuclear deal but are waiting for final US legislation that would lift the decades-old ban on the transfer of civilian nuclear technology and equipment to India. Germany has lately shown signs of softening its stance on the India-US nuclear deal and has indicated that it may support India in the powerful Nuclear Suppliers Group. But the Nordic countries, including Finland, have raised fears that countries like India are seeking global civilian nuclear commerce without signing the NPT.

Finally, the question of non-proliferation is closely connected with multilateralism. The great power aspirations of India are based on the hard power capabilities of a minimum nuclear deterrent and the soft power of a knowledge based economy. Indian policy makers favour an international system that rests no longer on a balance of power but on a "balance of interests".[18] Such concepts underline a more traditional great power approach in contrast to the EU. When it comes to the concrete politics of "effective multilateralism" there is a huge difference between wording and meaning. The EU favours an effective multilateralism that strengthens international organisations and the UN system. From a long term perspective, effective multilateralism aims at a stronger juridification of international relations. India on the other hand views multilateral institutions as fora for pursuing national interests. She therefore resists all attempts at external interference in internal affairs, not least with regard to the UN resolutions on Kashmir. This is why India refuses to join institutions like the International Criminal Court (ICC). Moreover India seems hesitant to

18. Address by External Affairs Minister on the occasion of National launch of Global India Foundation, *India and the Global Balance of Power.* In *http://meaindia.nic.in/speech/2007/01/16ss02.htm*

join the DAC consensus on development assistance because this again would bind India to some external norms that the government may share but is unwilling to follow. India's insistence on non-interference may also become a stumbling block in the negotiations for a EU-India free trade agreement. The EU is willing to include a clause relating to human rights and weapons of mass destruction which was refused by India.[19]

The different approaches are also obvious in the approach of both sides with regard to the Proliferation Security Initiative (PSI) a US-led political initiative launched in 2003 that seeks to increase cooperation among an informal grouping of member states, to curtail trafficking of weapons of mass destruction (WMD) on the seas, in the air and on the ground. Besides the US and Australia, PSI is supported by major EU countries like France, Germany, Italy, Japan, the Netherlands, Poland, Portugal, Spain, and the United Kingdom. The US have also indicated their interest that India should join the initiative although the country is not a member of the NPT. India has not yet decided whether it will participate in this kind of new security regime. One of the reservations of India may be that the PSI does not have backing from the UN. Moreover, India may fear that participation in such a "coalition of the willing" under US leadership would not be in accordance with the principles of an independent foreign policy.

EU-India Security Cooperation in the Making

The differences between India and the EU are more obvious with regard to international governance and multilateralism which reflect different foreign policy traditions. Indian policy makers favour a multipolar world in which India is one of the poles.[20] India emphasises the concept of national sovereignty and non-interference. Security cooperation between India and the EU is still in the making but offers an overall positive picture on the working level. Apart from their different legal international status both are international actors sharing many perceptions of security threats which will help deepen

19. Cronin, David (2007). "India-EU Deal Hits Political Rocks", In *Asia Times Online*. March 16 (accessed 17.3.07).

20. Ministry of Defence. *Annual Report 2005-06*. New-Delhi. p.2.

their collaboration. But one should not expect too much from this newly established strategic partnership. It should not be overlooked that aspects such as failing states, non-proliferation and multilateralism are embedded in different historical foreign policy traditions. At the same time, India is intensifying her military and defence cooperation with major EU member states like France, the United Kingdom and Germany. But the EU lacks military capabilities so far and puts therefore stronger emphasis on a soft power approach. It is therefore not astonishing that Indian security analysts do not perceive the EU as an important strategic player but are more oriented towards the US, Russia, China, and Japan.[21]

The EU nevertheless seems more innovative in its foreign policy approaches than India. It has for instance developed new mechanisms to deal with regional conflicts and failing states, like in Aceh or Sri Lanka. In contrast to this India pursues, because of her negative experiences in the past, a traditional approach of economic cooperation with failing states in her neighbourhood but has not yet developed a strategy of multilateral approaches for conflict resolution, besides UN peace-keeping missions. This is even more astonishing because India offers interesting resources for conflict mediation, for instance the capabilities of her Election Commission. So despite the common interest of the EU and India in supporting peace and reconstruction in conflict ridden countries like Sri Lanka, Nepal and Afghanistan both sides seem to pursue parallel activities rather than joint efforts. Does that all mean that EU-India security cooperation amounts to a policy of less risk and higher reward? Countries on India's rim have as much reason to welcome European influence as Europeans have to seek a role. For almost all of them, the EU is perceived as a soft power. And India wants closer ties with the EU as a means of diversifying risks.

The field of non-proliferation and multilateralism seems to be different. On the one hand the Indo-U.S. nuclear agreement has illustrated again problems for the EU in finding common positions against the national interests of its member states, i.e. France and the UK On the other hand with regard to new approaches like PSI India

21. Lisbonne-de Vergeron, Karine (2006). *Contemporary Indian Views of Europe.* London.

again is more hesitant to join such new initiatives in which major EU members participate. The concept of multilateralism may become another stumbling block because the EU's understanding of effective multilateralism aiming at a jurdification of international relations is in sharp contrast with India's view. Besides these differences both sides have enough commonalities for future cooperation in security issues from poverty and HIV to terrorism. Intensifying the security dialogue will be a first step that may help tackle more difficult areas in future.

10

India's Role in Regional Economic Integration in Asia

CLEMENS SPIESS

Introduction

While there is considerable buzz these days in the West over India's ascendancy in the global market place, the 'silent revolution' that is going on with regard to India's new role in regional economic integration in Asia gets much less attention. In mid-October 2005 an article in *The Hindu* quoted a government advisor as having said on the institutionalisation of India's trade and investment links with East Asia, "(...) if one looks at the prime minister's travel itinerary, most of it has been targeted at East and South-East Asia," and concluded that "(...) one of the tangible results has been a small horde of free trade agreements, completed or in the process of being negotiated."[1] These days, one can easily detect a new obsession with economic integration in India's foreign policy. And the main thrust of this obsession is a 'Look to the East'.

As compared to India's new enthusiasm when it comes to regional integration, the EU-India rapport somehow remains brittle and relatively inconsequential. This has a lot to do with India's resentment over Europe's reticence with regard to India's nuclear ambitions, its stand on tariff reduction in non-agricultural market access and other trade related issues, its restrictive policies on technology transfers and access of Indian professionals to the European labour market or the complexities of a policy rarely consistent with EU bureaucracy and administration. But, not the least, it is also due to a growing perception on the Indian side that the EU's days as an economic world

1. "The road bends here", *The Hindu*, October 17, 2005.

power are over, that, in the words of political analyst C. Raja Mohan, Europe is "(...) trapped between aggressive American capitalism and perceived Asian mercantilism."[2]

But what is it really about, this new Indian zest for regional economic integration in Asia? How far has India's economic interdependence with Asia already made headway? Since any analysis or, for that matter, critique of EU-India relations has to be aware of India's interest in regional (economic) integration and stand on her future economic and trade outlook, the following look into four dimensions of her new role in regional economic integration in Asia, namely her hitherto efforts at regional integration, her role in future scenarios of Asian economic integration, the "South Asian Association for Regional Cooperation" (SAARC) experience and the Sino-Indian relationship, can be worthwhile.

While the main focus of the following is on regional economic integration, the latter is always linked to the political dimension of regional integration and, consequently, the following will deal with both aspects of integration, the economic and the political.

India's Hitherto Role in Regional Economic Integration in Asia[3]

Until a couple of years ago India was not part, or, at least not an effective part, of any of the more relevant Asian efforts at regional economic integration. The gradual and unilateral liberalisation and domestic structural adjustments, which set in with the departure from her economic 'dirigisme' and the cautious opening up of her trade and, later on, investment regime in the early 1990s, had initially been accompanied only by free trade agreements with her South Asian neighbours, Nepal, Bhutan and Sri Lanka. Of these, the one with Nepal (and, to an extent, also the one with Bhutan) has to be seen in the light of the special historical relationship between a 'benevolent Indian paternalist' and a small, landlocked, traditional Himalayan kingdom, and only the more recent agreement with Sri Lanka can be

2. "Lessons in chemistry: why Blair may need to 'sex up' the India-Europe strategic cooperation", *Indian Express*, September 6, 2005.

3. See also Annexe 11.1.

considered as 'having paid off' in terms of a dividend in bilateral trade and an integrative output worth mentioning. On paper of course, there was, since the mid-1990s already, a preferential arrangement of SAARC-states, which eventually led to the inauguration of the first South Asian free trade agreement, SAFTA ('South Asian Free Trade Area') at the beginning of last year. However, for political, historical and economic reasons, which will be dealt with below, SAARC/SAFTA remains moribund and, even after more than twenty years of SAARC's existence, no real progress has been made with regard to either economic or political integration in the region.

Economically, South Asia is still the least integrated region worldwide (intra-regional trade adds up to only five per cent of the total exports of the region), not to mention the lack of a thorough political 'rapprochement' between SAARC—member states—despite the short-term paradigm shift in Indian foreign policy as declared in the Gujral-doctrine, which envisioned more friendly political relations with India's South Asian neighbours, except Pakistan.

In addition to the low degree of regional integration in South Asia itself, India was furthermore not able to secure membership in the prominent APEC ('Asia Pacific Economic Cooperation')—regime or the 'Asia-Europe-Meeting' (ASEM).

When only a couple of years after the founding of SAARC, it became clear that regional integration in South Asia would meet tremendous resistance, politically as well as economically, India devised and embarked upon its ambitious 'Look East Policy' designed to promote closer economic—and to a lesser degree also political—ties with the 'Association of South East Asian Nations' (ASEAN); meanwhile of course, the 'look to the East' policy comprises East Asia as well. It was obvious that, in the foreseeable future, the economies of Southeast and East Asia would be more complementary to India's own economic structure and trade patterns, and, that politically, progress in integration would be more feasible.

First, India became a sectoral, then a full dialogue partner of ASEAN; in 1996 India joined the 'ASEAN Regional Forum' (ARF), which discusses security related issues in the region, and since 2002 the country is involved in an ASEAN-plus-1 summit dialogue. Since two years now there is a framework agreement with ASEAN geared towards putting into practice an encompassing economic cooperation and free trade agreement.

Parallel to the establishment of closer ties with ASEAN the ,Bay of Bengal Initiative for Multi-Sectoral Technical and Economic Cooperation' (BIMSTEC) was launched, grouping together Bangladesh, India, Myanmar, Thailand and Sri Lanka (meanwhile Nepal and Bhutan have also joined). In 2004 India entered into a framework agreement with BIMSTEC similar to the one with ASEAN. While initially, BIMSTEC was also a strategic 'vehicle' to isolate Pakistan from efforts at regional integration or rather to circumvent Pakistan as an obstacle on the way to regional integration in South Asia, these days the main rationale of BIMSTEC from the Indian perspective is to serve as a 'bridge' between the South Asian and South East Asian economic spheres (for the same purpose the 'trilateral highway'—project was initiated furthering better infrastructural connectivity between India, Myanmar and Thailand).[4]

But it was only in the past couple of years—against the background of the formidable Indian economic boom, which necessitates conquering new markets and attracting investment,[5] and in the face of lessening political resistance to a further opening of her economy at home, the blocked multilateralism of the WTO and her desperate need as a resource-poor country to somehow secure the necessary inflow of oil and gas—, that India's new 'obsession' with regional (economic) integration began to unfold. In a sense, this obsession is also linked to the worldwide renaissance of processes of regional integration and the Indian fear not to 'miss the latest (economic) trend'.

Asia as the main thrust of India's new interest in regional integration—anyway part and parcel of her 'Look East' agenda—was the 'natural' choice, for trade with Asian countries, had risen to one-

4. The 'Mekong-Ganga Cooperation Grouping' (MGC, comprising India, Myanmar, Vietnam, Thailand, Cambodia and Laos) or the 'Bangladesh-China-India Myanmar Forum' (CIM) are other such regional initiatives designed to promote closer linkages between the respective member states in the region.

5. Not only, or not primarily because of its dependence on the global market as the prime off shoring destination of the world in the IT-service sector and, increasingly, in financial services or Business Process Outsourcing (BPO) as well, but also in order to overhaul and expand its poor infrastructure and to make inroads into other industries.

third of India's total trade volume in the course of the country's liberalisation (Asia—seen as a whole—has meanwhile overtaken the EU and the USA as India's main trading partner) and countries such as Japan, South Korea, the ASEAN-states and, above all, China had developed into her most dynamic economic and trading partners.

Bilateral free trade agreements with Thailand (2003) and Singapore (2005) were signed, other agreements with Japan, South Korea, Malaysia and China are in the pipe line. The preferential arrangement with Afghanistan (2003) has to be seen in the light of India's efforts to integrate Afghanistan into SAARC and to counterbalance Pakistani influence on Afghanistan. A free trade agreement with Bangladesh, India's biggest South Asian trading partner, is in the making.

Following the proclamation by then Indian Foreign Minister Yashwant Sinha, in 2002, that India's future agenda of her economic South-South diplomacy would be "(...) to work out a road map which, within a fixed time frame, will ultimately lead us to a free-trade arrangement with all regional groups of developing countries (...),"[6] the last couple of years saw the signing of preferential agreements and framework agreements for close economic and trade cooperation with Chile, the South African Customs Union, MERCOSUR and the Gulf Region. A preferential agreement in the context of the IBSA-initiative (the loose strategic alliance comprising India, South Africa and Brazil) is currently discussed.

Altogether however, and despite the signing of a plethora of new bilateral or regional trade agreements, India—comparable to Asia as a region, perhaps with the exception of the ASEAN—is only at the beginning of a process of profound and thorough regional integration.

Almost all of the Indian trade agreements, perhaps with the exception of the one with Singapore, are examples of what is termed 'shallow integration', with no substantial tariff reduction and a restriction to a gradual liberalisation of trade in goods. In no case one could talk of 'deep integration', the hallmark of the EU and other established and institutionalised arrangements of regional integration,

6. "India's Foreign Policy: Successes, Failures and Visions in the Changing World Order", speech by Foreign Minister Yashwant Sinha at the National Defence College, New Delhi, 18 November 2002; available at: *http://www.meadev.nic.in/speeches/stmt-eam-nationaldefen.htm*

going beyond trade regulations to comprise investment, services, product standards, technical regulations, competition policy or even labour and environmental standards etc. (on paper, SAARC has a lot of declarations and statements announcing its intention to move towards such a 'deep integration', inclusive of a Social Charter, in practice however, the future of regional integration, especially in South Asia, is written in the stars.)

One can conclude that Asia wide, the existing 81 different regional trade and free trade agreements as well as the 52 free trade agreements currently under negotiation are all more or less market-driven, geared towards establishing production-sharing regimes, and are hardly of an institutional nature and thus the result of sustainable policy-making. In addition, the plethora of only loosely coordinated bilateral free trade agreements that characterises regional integration in Asia today can reinforce the potentially harmful 'noodle bowl effect', whereby the complexity of the different rules of origin arising from many overlapping agreements among members of different trade arrangements increases transaction costs and, consequently, acts as a deterrent for trade and investment.

India and Future Scenarios of Asian Economic Integration

Against the background of Asia catching up with other regions of the world in terms of regional integration and the ‚new regionalism' worldwide, which, in principle, undermines the multilateralism of the WTO, but is politically more feasible, a new kind of Asian enthusiasm for integration has developed, in which India is playing an increasingly decisive role when it comes to contemplating future scenarios of regional integration.

Contrary to her past credo for multilateralism India has also become less flexible at the WTO-bargaining table and is increasingly pursuing a double strategy: on the one hand closely allied to various pressure groups of developing countries and emerging markets, especially when it comes to agrarian interests and the reduction of subsidies in the North, on the other hand safeguarding its own interests as an upcoming economic major power when it comes to negotiating services or copyrights.

In the face of growing disappointment with the WTO as an instrument or institutional device for promoting an effective multilateralism and simultaneous economic dynamism in Asia the Indian or rather Asian zest for regional integration is therefore only logical. In that regard, one should not forget that from the Indian/ Asian perspective, the Western demand for a multilateral approach takes place also against the background of established zones of regional integration of the West (EU, NAFTA) not losing a competitive advantage.

India's official interest in regional integration, reflected in her rhetoric, is aimed at the establishment of a pan-Asian free trade zone, or 'Asian Economic Community' (AEC). As Prime Minister Manmohan Singh indicated in 2004: "(...) we envision an Asian Economic Community, which encompasses ASEAN, China, Japan, Korea and India (...) This community of nations would constitute an 'arc of advantage', across which there would be large-scale movement of people, capital, ideals and creativity."[7]

For the moment, the basic idea behind the vision is to bring together the main economic blocs in East, South East and South Asia in an all-encompassing free trade zone comprising Japan, ASEAN, China, India and South Korea, a zone, which is meanwhile commonly known as the 'JACIK community' (one could also talk of ASEAN-plus-4). Further thoughts include Australia and New Zealand as well. In 2003 this community, which seems to converge with the ideas of the East Asian and ASEAN countries to form an 'East Asian Community' (EAC), had a total population of over 3 billion people, a gross national income in purchasing power parity of 16 billion US $ and international reserves of 1.6 billion US $—and would have been an economic centre of gravity only comparable to the EU and NAFTA.[8] Eventually, JACIK would force other Asian economies to join, thus eliminating the above mentioned 'noodle-bowl effect'.

---

7. Prime Minister Manmohan Singh's speech at the *Third India-ASEAN Business Summit*, 21 October 2004; available at: *http://pmindia.nic.in/speech/content.asp?id=35*

8. See: Annexe 11.2 and Kumar, Nagesh. "Towards a Broader Asian Community: Agenda for the East Asia Summit." RIS (Research and Information System for the Non-Aligned and other Developing Countries) Discussion Paper No. 100, 2005; and Asher, Mukul G and Rahul Sen. India-East Asia Integration. A Win-Win for Asia. RIS (Research and Information System for the Non-Aligned and other Developing Countries) Discussion Paper No. 91, 2005

And it seems that the incorporation of India into the envisioned EAC is also a priority of East and South East Asian countries, if one is to judge from the enthusiastic receipt India got at the first 'East Asia Summit', held in Kuala Lumpur at the end of 2005. Especially the ASEAN-states, Japan and South Korea would welcome India as a potential counterweight to perceived Chinese dominance. India is however rather sceptical as far as the political dimension of pan-Asian integration is concerned.

There are two alternative scenarios to this quasi-pan-Asian free trade community: 1) a 'Hub and Spokes'-bilateralism, whereby a regional economic hegemon (the 'hub')—meaning China, ASEAN or India—is connected with peripheral states/economies (the 'spokes') through a web of bilateral free trade agreements. In the most extreme case of this scenario there would be only limited market access among the 'spokes', so that the 'hub' or 'centre', would have considerable economic advantage; and 2) the development of two sub-regional areas of integration in East and South Asia, which would be connected with each other through bilateral free trade agreements.[9] From the Indian perspective however, both scenarios seem to be neither favourable nor realistic.

India is still not that much of a prominent or relevant market for Asian trade flows, especially in comparison to China, but also Japan, South Korea and the ASEAN. The same holds true for a South Asian free trade zone in comparison to an East Asian one, so that either in the 'Hub-and-Spokes'-scenario or in the second one, an extremely asymmetrical economic weighting would be created. Additionally, the second scenario would require a more or less smooth implementation of regional integration in South Asia, something, which, despite the existence of SAARC and the inauguration of SAFTA, is less than realistic.

SAARC—The Missed Opportunity

Of course, a take-off of regional integration in South Asia would be desirable and highly necessary, maybe less so because of mere

9. See: Wang, JiangYu, 'China, India, and Regional Economic Integration in Asia' (June 2006). Available at Social Sciences Research Network: *http://ssrn.com/abstract=924700*

economic reasons, but for security related reasons and where conflict prevention is concerned—as well as against the background of the question of energy security and the sharing of natural resources.

So far, the balance sheet of SAARC in terms of integration is however, rather meagre and the SAFTA-agenda, which envisions to start with the reduction of trade barriers and tariffs now, to establish a South Asian free trade zone by 2010 and to create a customs union by 2015 and an economic union by 2020, unfortunately has to be dismissed as a mere rhetorical concept..

Particularly as, from a trade perspective, SAFTA presently factors out Indo-Pakistani trade, is mainly restricted to trade of goods (there is no service dimension) and will probably contain a plethora of exceptions from tariff reduction and complex/complicated rules of origin because of the similar trade patterns of member states. With the exception of the smaller member states such as Nepal, Bhutan and the Maldives, there is also no real economic imperative for deeper economic integration or rather a liberalisation of intra-regional trade, which is anyway only marginal.[10]

This is especially so for India, which represents roughly 70 per cent of the total SAARC market and without which no progress in integration can take place. Largely for historical reasons export structures are too similar (agrarian products, textiles); and the resistance from domestic industries is simply too big. At the same time, the dynamism of the bilateral free trade agreement between India and Sri Lanka shows that trade/export patterns can change in favour of intra-regional trade, and there are of course areas beyond trade in goods (services, banking, and investments) where complementarities exist.

The biggest obstacle on the way towards deepening regional integration in South Asia is however the stalemate political conflicts and the often precarious state of governance and government—above all the more than half a century old Indo-Pak conflict, but also political crises in Nepal and Bangladesh and resurgent civil war in Sri Lanka.

10. See: *South Asian Free Trade Area. Opportunities and Challenges.* A USAID Report, 2005. Available at: *www.afghanistan-mfa.net/RECC/712_SAFTA_Report_Opportunities_and_ Challenges.pdf.*

Since its inception, SAARC has been characterised by a strong connection between its economic and political dimension and almost all of its member states were pursuing a specific political agenda when joining, an agenda arising out of historical antagonisms and the implications of the region's distinct territoriality—the smaller states' fear of Indian dominance and India's perception of her South Asian neighbours as an integral part of the Indian sphere of influence. Although India is increasingly aware, that not only or, for that matter, not necessarily for the sake of economic benefit[11], but basically for the sake of her own security interests[12] and in view of the much-needed energy security and the many pipeline projects (Iran-Pakistan-India, Burma-Bangladesh-India) as well as considering the fact that a less conflict ridden relationship with its South Asian neighbours would enhance its standing in the international system and reduce its military expenditure, she has to push ahead regional cooperation and integration.[13]

In her policy towards her neighbours however, ad hoc-bilateralism and reserve still largely prevail. In this context, the concession to add to the SAARC Charter the possibility of discussing and resolving bilateral conflicts at the regional level, could be a first step towards using SAARC as a vehicle for political integration.

India and China: A New Axis?[14]

At present, the most interesting development with regard to Asian integration is without doubt the 'rapprochement' between India and China. Given the Delhi visits of Chinese Premier Wen Jiabao in spring 2005 and of Chinese President Hu Jintao in November 2006, the

11. For example through intensified trade relations with Pakistan or improved trade and transport linkages between her (backward) north-eastern States and Bangladesh.
12. With regard to infiltration of militants from Pakistan, Indian insurgent groups operating from Bangladesh, Nepali Maoists and Indian Naxalites, trying to establish a 'red corridor' stretching from Nepal through Bihar to Andhra Pradesh, cross-border activities of Sri Lankan and Indian Tamils etc.
13. Nevertheless, the economic rationale is also a strong motivator of India's current advocacy of regional integration. As Prime Minister Singh said in November 2005: "(...) given the strong trends towards economic integration which go far beyond tariff reductions to gradual economic convergence, any region can ignore the formation of its own scheme of regional integration only at its own peril." See: 'SAARC at 20: will the future be different?', *The Hindu*, November 11, 2005.
14. See also the article by Mohan and Voll in this volume.

cooperation agreements signed during these visits in the name of the strategic partnership of both countries, the opening of the Nathu-La pass in Sikkim for trading goods in the summer of 2006 (more of a symbolic gesture) and the framework agreement to solve the decade old border disputes, the old slogan of "*Hindi Chini Bhai Bhai*" from the days of Nehru and Zhou En-lai, before the Sino-Indian border war of 1962, seems to have come alive again—this is of course not the case, not yet at least. However, discussions regarding the creation of a Sino-Indian free trade agreement, fuelled by the rise of China as India's second biggest trade partner and accompanied by political concessions, are real. Remembering that the Indian nuclear tests of 1998 were justified by the 'China fear' (also out of strategic interest) this development could almost be called 'spectacular'.

The question remains how realistic is such a development towards a free trade agreement and how the different perspectives on the Sino-Indian thaw look like. A look at the macroeconomic data and basic trade figures of both countries[15] makes clear that China is still way ahead of India with regard to all important indicators (GDP, trade volume, share of world trade, Foreign Direct Investments)—this holds true for the still much higher degree of protectionism of the Indian trade regime. Only when it comes to services trade and with regard to the dynamism (not volume) of growth in merchandise trade, especially with East Asian countries, India is quickly catching up.[16] This asymmetry is also reflected in bilateral trade. While China is getting more and more important for India as a trade partner, the volume of trade with India adds up to less than 1.5 per cent of China's total foreign trade volume; India is currently China's tenth biggest trade partner. And, while the Chinese export basket is diversified and of high quality (dominated by machines and consumer goods), the Indian one is mainly restricted to commodities (cotton and ores) and only about five Indian products have attained considerable market penetration in China. Also the much cited complementarity of Indian

---

15. See Annexe 10.3.

16. See: Asher, Mukul G. and Rahul Sen (2005). "India-East Asia Integration. A Win-Win for Asia", *Discussion Paper* No. 91. RIS (Research and Information System for the Non-Aligned and other Developing Countries)

software and Chinese hardware, so far has not led to considerable synergy effects and mutual investments are still only marginal.

The clear imbalance in Sino-Indian economic relations finds its expression furthermore in the mood of the Indian business community, which is still very sceptical about a possible free trade agreement fearing the comparative advantage of China and the flooding of the Indian market with cheap Chinese products. From the Chinese perspective it is mainly high opportunity costs like, for example, the (often politically motivated) laborious and long-drawn-out licence and permit procedures or visa permissions, which stand in the way of a stronger Chinese engagement in India. Many Chinese investment plans were called off by Indian authorities in the name of national security. Even though many Indians concede that competition with China, induced by a free trade agreement, would stimulate the necessary expansion of labour-intensive industries and that India can 'learn a lot' from China—as becomes visible from the current controversy about the introduction of 'Special Economic Zones' (SEZ) emulating the Chinese model, a controversy, which also demonstrates the differences of economic reforms in a democratic and in an authoritarian environment—so far mutual distrust and an attitude of cautious reserve still largely prevail.

This is above all due to the politically burdened and conflict-laden history of Sino-Indian relations; the political resistance to a relationship tied too closely is still very pronounced, especially on the Indian side. The Indian security establishment eyes with suspicion the Chinese engagement in India's neighbouring countries, especially Pakistan, but also Bangladesh and Myanmar. There is a lot of talk about the 'string of pearls', with which China tries to expand its sphere of influence around India.

The Sino-Indian 'rapprochement' has to be understood against a geopolitical background as well. India seeks China's goodwill and support with regard to the approaching decision of the 'Nuclear Suppliers Group' about the Indo-US nuclear deal and, in the long run, also with regard to India's interest in a seat in the UN Security Council. And, it still has to be understood as some sort of a 'Confidence-Building Measure'—a far-reaching economic interdependence and a close political relationship are still miles away.

Anyway, the solution to the border disputes between India and China in the Himalayas is a crucial litmus test, standing in the way of closer political relations. The Chinese recognition of Sikkim as an integral part of the Indian Union and the Indian recognition of Tibet as an autonomous region of China have paved the way for such a solution, an agreement on disputed territories in Ladakh and Himachal Pradesh seems to be within range.

The statement of the Chinese ambassador in Delhi shortly before the visit of Hu Jintao, that not only the disputed border region of Tawang, but, in principle, the whole Indian State of Arunachal Pradesh belongs to China, showed however, how far one is still away from a breakthrough on the border issue. The indignation in Delhi about this statement was considerable and a lot of diplomatic effort behind the scenes was necessary to turn the Chinese President's visit into a success.

Annexe 10.1

India's Regional Trade Agreements

	Title	Scope	Type	Status	Year
APTA	Asia-Pacific Trade Agreement (previously known as the Bangkok Agreement)	Regional	Non-reciprocal Agreement	In force since	1975
ASEANINDFA on	ASEAN–India Framework Agreement on Comprehensive Economic Cooperation	Country–Bloc	Framework Agreement	In force since	2004
BHUINDFTA	Bhutan–India Free Trade Agreement	Bilateral	Free Trade Agreement	In force since	1995
BIMSTEC	Bay of Bengal Initiative for Multi-Sectorial Technical and Economic Cooperation (BIMSTEC)	Regional Agreement	Framework	In force since	2004
INDAFGPTA	India-Afghanistan Preferential Trade Agreement	Bilateral	Preferential Arrangement	In force since	2003
INDCHNPTA	India–Chile Preferential Trade Agreement	Cross–Continental BilateralTrade	Preferential Agreement	Under negotiation since	2005
INDGCCFA	India–Gulf Cooperation Council (GCC) Framework Agreement	Country–Bloc	Framework Agreement	In force since	2004
INDLKABTA	India–Sri Lanka Bilateral Trade Agreement	Bilateral	Free Trade Agreement	In force since	2001

contd...

...contd...

	Title	*Scope*	*Type*	*Status*	*Year*
INDMERCPTA	India–Mercosur Preferential Trade Agreement	Country–Bloc	Framework Agreement	Pending country ratification	2005
INDNPLTOT	India–Nepal Indo-Nepal Treaty of Trade	Bilateral	Non-reciprocal Agreement	In force since	1991
INDSACUTA	India–South African Customs Union (SACU) Trade Agreement	Country–Bloc	Preferential Trade Agreement	Under negotiation since	2002
INDSGPCECA	India–Singapore Comprehensive Economic Cooperation Agreement	Bilateral	Free Trade Agreement	In force since	2005
INDTHAFA	India–Thailand Framework Agreement for establishing a FTA	Bilateral	Framework Agreement	In force since	2003
SAFTA	South Asian Association for Regional Cooperation Free Trade Arrangement (SAFTA)	Regional	Free Trade Agreement	In force since	2006
SAPTA	SAARC Preferential Trading Arrangement (SAPTA)	Regional	Preferential Arrangement	In force since	1995

Source: Wang, JiangYu, 'China, India, and Regional Economic Integration in Asia' (June 2006). Available at Social Sciences Research Network: *http://ssrn.com/abstract=924700*. Compiled from UNESCAP: Online Preferential Trade Agreements Database in Asia and the Pacific, other sources for up-dates

Annexe 10.2

Proposed East Asian or JACIK Community in Relation to European Union and NAFTA in 2003

(billion US $)

	EU	*NAFTA*	*JACIK (14)*	*JACIK-AN (16)*
Gross National Income, PPP (in Purchasing Power Parity)	10137	12847	16058	16716
% of World total	20.14	25.53	31.91	33.22
GDP	10505	12431	7262	8198
% of World total	29.37	34.76	21.24	22.92
Exports (2002)	3523	1486	1657	1757
% of World total	46.50	19.62	21.88	23.20
International Reserves	285	170	1657	1757
Population (millions)	381	425	3065	3089
% of World total	6.12	6.83	49.27	49.65

Source: Kumar, Nagesh. *Towards a Broader Asian Community: Agenda for the East Asia Summit*. RIS (Research and Information System for the Non-Aligned and other Developing Countries) Discussion Paper No. 100, 2005, p. 9. Compiled from World Bank, *World Development Indicators 2005*,CD-ROM; IMF, *International Financial Statistics 2004*.

Annexe 10.3

China and India: Economic and Trade Indicators Compared

		China		India	
		2001	*2005*	*2001*	*2005*
GDP (US$ bn)		1324.8	2224.9	478.3	803.3
GDP Growth Rate (%)		8.3	9.9	5.8	8.1
GNI Per capita (US$)		1000	1700	460	– (620 in 2004)
Value of Trade in Goods (US$ bn)	Exports Imports	266.2 243.6	762 660.1	43.6 49.6	89.8 131.6
Share in World Trade in Goods (%)	Exports Imports	4.3 3.8	7.3 6.1	0.7 0.8	0.9 1.2
Annual Percentage Change: Goods (%)	Exports Imports	7 8	28 18	3 -3	19 35
Value of Trade in Commercial Service (US$ bn)	Exports Imports	32.9 39.0	81.2 85.3	20.4 23.4	68 67
Share in World Trade in Services (%)	Exports Imports	2.3 2.7	3.4 3.6	1.4 1.6	2.8 2.9
Annual Percentage Change: Services (%)	Exports Imports	9 9	31 19	15 19	76 73
Rank in World Trade: Goods	Exports Imports	6 6	3 3	30 27	29 17
Rank in World Trade: Services	Exports Imports	12 10	8 7	19 18	10 10
Foreign Direct Investment (US$ bn)		46.8	60.3	4.7	5.3
Foreign Exchange Reserves (US$ bn)		212.2	820	51	137.4
Tariff Binding Coverage (%)			100		73.8
Bound Tariff (%)			10.0		49.8
Applied Tariff (%)			10.4		29.1
Share of MFN Duty Free Imports			34.0		2.1
GATS Services Sectors with Commitments			93		37

Note: EU is not counted as a single trader and hence intra-EU trade is not excluded.

Source: Wang, Jiang Yu (2006). "China, India, and Regional Economic Integration in Asia". June. Available at Social Sciences Research Network: *http://ssrn.com/abstract=924700*. Compiled from The Economist Intelligence Unit, World Bank, Asian Development Bank, World Trade Organization, International Monetary Fund.

11

The Emancipation of Indian Dalits from a European Perspective

KLAUS JULIAN VOLL and HANS-GEORG WIECK

The Dalit-issue[1] that continues to plague the Indian nation is well known—in India itself and abroad. Many Indian citizens as well as considerable parts of the international community, sometimes much to the chagrin of the Government of India, are concerned. There is practically no doubt whatsoever in the public awareness regarding India that there is still a great deal of social discrimination[2] and deprivation of the approximately 160 million Dalits and another 60 to 80 millions *Adivasis*—literally the "original inhabitants", in India officially called "Scheduled Tribes"—existing, besides an awareness that this deplorable state of affairs is in gross violation of the Indian Constitution of January 26, 1950. Undoubtedly, the political leadership of the country, the "leadership" of relevant institutions are fully aware about the undeniable fact that in future even more substantial funds have to be allocated, in order to alleviate the fate of these fellow citizens, which constitute altogether nearly one fourth of the population.[3] A great deal of efforts are undertaken to overcome these deficiencies—but will this support for the Dalit cause be in place in time, since they are predominantly the victims of hunger and

---

1. This means the "oppressed or excluded" as the officially so-called "Scheduled Castes" (SC's) increasingly prefer to call themselves. The term "Harijans" ("Children of God"), euphemistically coined by Mahatma Gandhi, is not any longer acceptable and increasingly regarded as derogatory.
2. Hahn, Walter (2006). "The Platform "Dalit Solidarity in Germany" (DSID): Activities and the Internet", in Klaus Voll and Doreen Beierlein (eds.), *Rising India – Europe's Partner? Foreign and Security Policy, Politics, Economics, Human Rights and Social Issues.* Berlin, New Delhi: Media, Civil Society and Intercultural Dimensions. pp.716-726
3. There is no dearth of well-documented figures and descriptions about the atrocities against Dalits and other weaker sections of Indian society, compare for instance Debroy, Bibek and Shyam Babu (2005). *The Dalit Question – Reforms and Social Justice.* New Delhi: Globus Books.

malnutrition?![4] Or will the funds once again end up in other people's purses as, is unfortunately so often the case?

Besides official institutions like the National Commission on Human Rights, organisations like the Indian Institute of Dalit Studies (IIDS), the latter erstwhile under the patronage of the late President of India, K. R. Narayanan, a Dalit by social background, and interestingly initially funded by the American Ford Foundation, as well as the Jesuite Indian Social Institute (ISI) do provide sufficient materials.

Socially committed Social Sciences and area studies about India, be it by European, other international—such as members of the International Dalit Solidarity Committee—or Indian authors have to develop comprehensive analytical tools and categories in order to express and substantiate adequately the plight of the Indian people[5], of which Dalits form quite a significant part, thereby exercising also some intellectual pressure on the Indian Government and dominating sections of society, including sections of India's intelligentsia. If we mention the "suffering of large parts of the Indian people", we recollect in reconstructive comparison phenomena like "pauperism", with its implications of hunger and malnutrition affecting sections of the European populace in the 18th and early 19th centuries, as described and analysed in the works of August Bebel, Eduard Bernstein, Charles Dickens, Norbert Elias, Hartmut Elsenhans, Friedrich Engels, Eric Hobsbawm, Karl Kautyky, Karl Marx, Thomas Nipperdey and Hans-Ulrich Wehler amongst others.

Europe' Heritage as a Model?

What has Europe historically and what have the different major European states and sections of their societies nowadays really to do with the situation of Dalits, particularly under the process of increased globalisation? Is it only an academic or at best a philosophical interest, emanating from tenets of the era of enlightenment and the French revolution, based on the assumption of the basic equality of all human

4. Drèze, Jean (2006). "Democracy and The Right to Food", in Voll and Beierlein *op. cit.* p.727-50
5. Voll, Klaus (2005). "The Failure of Governance—Politics, Sociology and the Perspectives of Food Insecurity in India", in Uwe Kracht, Manfred Schulz (eds.), *Food and Nutrition Security in the Process of Globalization and Urbanization*. Muenster: LIT. pp. 702-11.

beings irrespective of their social status, gender, colour and religion, articulated by nostalgic proponents of universal human rights from good "old" Europe? In general, Europe achieved the social and educational modernisation of the working class, also through health and insurance systems, respectively educational institutions like the "People's High-Schools" ("*Volks-Hochschulen*") in Germany. Hans-Eberhard Dingels, between 1961 till 1995 International Secretary of the Social Democratic Party of Germany (SPD), stresses the contribution of Jewish intellectuals, amongst other functions as Editors-in-Chief of the influential party press, and their impact on the emancipation of the working-class and Trade Union movement in their struggles against such oddities as the German Officers Class and the remnants of the medieval system of guilds in the process of industrialisation.

Historically, the so-called "lower" sections of European societies and their respective political outfits, particularly in such core-countries as England, France and Germany, have played, during the transition to predominantly industrialised economies, a major role in the processes of democratisation and public education. Is it here, with a certain historical delay, that corresponding developments like a "silent revolution" and a "second democratic upsurge" can be observed in the Indian context since the 80's of the last century and can there, irrespective of the numerous social, political and cultural differences, some general similarities be observed, without neglecting earlier emancipatory social and educational movements in India even during colonial times? Before addressing some of the similarities, we should realise the fundamental difference of the social and political potential of the "working class" during the period of mechanical industrialisation in Europe and North America and the fact that the Dalits and *Adivasis* were and to an extent are the "product" of religiously proclaimed exclusion, deprivation and discrimination. The labour force was indispensable for the industrial development of the then emerging industialised countries and therefore constituted a political force to reckon with. Social-Democrats represented for decades the largest parliamentary party in the German Reichstag of Imperial Germany between 1871 until 1918. Bismarck's social legislation towards the end of the 19th century was meant to curb the growing strength of the

Social-Democrats. Compared to this situation, Dalits were of a relatively marginal social and economic importance for Indias' overall economic development, although they continue to contribute to the processes of "original accumulation" as farm and child labourers etc. They constituted—together with other segments of the population—a "burden" from the point of view of those who created a system of "structural force" for them and they were living on the basis of subsistence—as they do still in large numbers today.

At the political level, the Dalit parties that finally emerged as a result of gradual social and professional progress among Dalits with all their regional and internal differentiations, brought about by their quota shares in education and access to state jobs, don't possess the economic expertise and visions for instance of the erstwhile *Social Democratic Party* in the second half of the 19th and the beginning of the 20th century. Till date, they lack a deeper competence and therefore explanatory capability to thoroughly understand the complicated nature of the Indian power system, e.g. the nature of the "democratically legitimised State Class with its growing criminal and plutocratic tendencies", the economic and societal foundations and basic interests of the Indian bourgeoisie[6] and middle classes. Some insiders maintain, that the leadership of the Bahujan Samaj Party (BSP), currently the most powerful Dalit party, is actually adverse to a too comprehensive intellectual and economic expertise, although it harbours the potential for a social-democratic political movement with nascent signs of a people's party, at least in Uttar Pradesh as far as the social composition of party candidates for the 2007 State Assembly elections in this most populous Indian state have been concerned. The overwhelming success of the BSP with an unexpected absolute majority could strengthen such tendencies.

Dalits, irrespective of such outstanding personalities as Dr. Ambedkar,[7] K.R. Narayanan or Kanshi Ram and their rise to prominent positions, have not yet reached the stage, where their urge for identity and emancipation has led to mass phenomena like the *"Von der Wiege bis zur Bahre"*, e.g. a life-long learning endeavour from

6. Compare Rajghatt Chidanand and Agencies. "India Pips Japan in Super-rich List", *The Times of India*, 10-3-07. p.1. India has the highest amount of Dollar billionaires in Asia.

7. Jaffrelot, Christophe (2004). *Dr. Ambedkar and Untouchability.* New Delhi: Permanent Book.

the cradle to the grave, which has been so characteristic for the early working class movement in Germany. Instead, organisations like the Dalit Sena ("Army of Dalits") did not have the visible impact as for instance its illustrious founder Ram Vilas Paswan, one of India's most prominent Dalit politicians and a long-time Cabinet Minister, wants to make us believe, easily at hand with possibly very exaggerated figures.

The Social Welfare State in Europe is under severe constraints. For instance in Germany, income and wealth gaps are constantly increasing, although Social Democrats have been leading a coalition Government for seven years and are since the 2005 elections the junior partner in a so-called "Grand Coalition." But nevertheless, the heritage of the general and legal equality of all human beings is undisputed, without any insinuations of "untouchability" and "racial inferiority" ascribed to any segment of society.

Truth and Reconciliation Conference of Dalits and Caste Hindus

In the past, India has generated any amount of founders of religions, seers, saints and godmen, sometimes with tremendous political influence, and is definitely producing the latter variety also in present times. Sri Sri Ravi Shankar, himself revered by his followers as "His Holiness", is the founder of the Art of Living Foundation, which is allegedly working in 25,000 villages, but he is above all internationally well connected, with a claimed outreach to approximately 3 million people in about 151 countries, also in affiliation with the UN system. He organised on the 9th of March 2007 a Truth and Reconciliation Conference of Dalits and Caste Hindus in the Hamsadhvani Stadium, Pragati Maidan in New Delhi, attended by about 2,000 people. The long list of the names of the Participating Organisations and Communities, more than 50 altogether and all with caste-based identities, revealed the true nature of the ensemble of Indian (sub-) societies and reads like a veritable Who is Who of Indian Castes and their representative organisations. This event gave the lie to all those who do not consider caste identity as the determining one in contemporary India and instead propagate all-embracing identities like class, gender or religion as more comprehensive ones. The tremendously complicated, covert and manifold masked Indian society contains also a System of Apartheid.[8] Therefore, one has to envisage the emancipatory efforts of all social sections and especially of *Dalits* outside the upper-caste system within these parameters also.

"The house is on fire", so said R. Shankar, advocating "a peace which will bring a revolution and lead to a unified and beautiful society." He referred to the historical contributions of Dalits and other representatives of so-called "lower sections" to the formulation of classical texts of Hindu (*Sanatan*) literature. "Moving away from Hinduism and converting to other religions has not helped Dalits in their war against the oppressive caste system. Past wrongs cannot be undone through anger and rage. ...Both Dalits and other caste Hindus have to change.... It is time for reconciliation. If it doesn't happen now, society will reel in cycles of revenge and counter-revenge. For justice and progress, there has to be reconciliation."[9]

The 7-point action Plan, acclaimed by the participants, propagates the following: "1. Temple entry for Dalits 2. Collective celebration including community feasts 3. Abolition of separate utensils for Dalits 4. Empowerment of women from economically weaker sections of society 5. Providing educational facilities especially to weaker sections of society 6. Providing spiritual and religious education to Dalit children, which they have been deprived of for hundreds of years 7. Equality and justice for one and all without any discrimination."[10]

At this stage it is not evident, if this effort, besides the expressed fear about the potential erosion of Hindu Society and the attempts to avoid this process, did serve also a political purpose, since Shri Agarwal, Member of Parliament of the Hindu nationalist Bharatiya Janata Party (BJP) and President of the All India Vaish Federation[11] as well as Udit Raj, President of the Indian Justice Party and also of the All-India Federation of Scheduled Castes and Scheduled Tribes Employees, participated. U. Raj interestingly maintained, that India could not become a world power, if internal divisions would not be eradicated. "You have all to drink poison, entrenched in our society."

8. See a very comprehensive little booklet from the 1980's of a Bangalore based Dalit organisation with the topic "Apartheid in India".
9. Extract from the invitation leaflet for this conference.
10. Ibid.
11. *Vaishya* do constitute the *Banya* or trader caste.

He stressed that not a single Dalit could be found in the list of India's one thousand leading entrepreneurs and that Dalits could not expect help from upper-castes. A Brahmin representative, who stated that in his organisation's temple in Patna the headpriest is a Dalit, claimed that the upliftment of Dalits would be instrumental to make India a super-power. Members of the Paswan[12] community maintained, that the 7-point programme is not anymore relevant for their people and that economic empowerment has gained the highest priority. He referred to the far more precise and sophisticated "Bhopal Declaration" with regard to the empowerment of Dalits. It has to be seen, if this conference, "organised against resistance", really constituted a "historic event for the transformation of India", as claimed by Ravi Shankar. Interestingly, in the long list of social and religious reformers in India mentioned by him, he particularly referred to Gautama Buddha.

Short-sightedness of the Elite and the Middle Classes or Deliberate Discrimination?

The all-pervasive argument in so many socially oriented discussions in India is: "India is too poor to afford all this", like universal primary education, overcoming hunger and malnutrition, rampant hazardous and less hazardous child labour[13] etc. But original capital accumulation in India, like historically in Germany and other European states, does also take place to a certain degree on the backs of the rural populace and the urban marginalised.[14]

Given the fast capital accumulation, as a result of the continuous high growth rates particularly during the last few years, but already starting in the 1980's, the above argument, which was already not true in the past, does not carry conviction anymore. In the past, one could wonder, why even fairly enlightened members of the upper and middle classes and castes resorted to these evasive statements and wasted unnecessarily so much mental and intellectual energy. Prime Minister

---

12. Dalits in parts of Bihar.
13. Gupta, Manju and Klaus Voll (1999). "Child Labour in India: An Exemplary Case Study", in Klaus Voll (ed.), *Child Labour. Indian and International Dimensions and Strategies*. New Delhi: Mosaic Books.
14. Köberlein, Michael (2003). *Living from Waste. Livelihoods of the Actors Involved in Delhi's Informal Waste Recycling Economy.* Saarbrücken: Verlag für Entwicklungspolitik.

Dr. Manmohan Singh, asked about the reasons for the still low literacy rates, by any international standards, once stated: "I have come to the conclusion that the high amount of illiteracy in this country is a conspiracy of the elite."[15]

With the rise of new segments in India's entrepreneurial bourgeoisie, such impeccable and utmost successful modernisers in the field of Information Technology like Azim Premji and S. Narayana Murthy, the latter articulates sophisticated visions for a comprehensive industrialisation strategy, do mince no words in analysing these structural deficits of India's society, economy and political decision mechanisms with regard to the lack of adequate primary education, thereby reducing the full usage of India's manpower potential, particularly also in view of the lack of wide-spread vocational training. In this regard, Azim Premji is outspoken with very clear arguments. It is so evident and can be permanently experienced in daily life, that India requires large scale functional vocational training programmes. This could facilitate the political intention of job reservations for Dalits and other disadvantaged sections also in the private sector of the Indian economy. The productive energies of these deprived and at the same time aspiring Indian citizens, could turn into a tremendous asset during India's "belated industrial revolution" with its growing influence on the world economy.

Historically, Germany's industrial revolution in the 19th century benefited also a lot from the introduction of universal primary education and the final abolition of child labour in a process covering several decades.[16] The rise of the labour movement, its own educational efforts ("From the cradle to the grave") and the formation of a unified "Social Democratic Party of Germany", contributed in a long-drawn out process towards an essential challenge to the intellectual and economic hegemony of the German bourgeoisie and its allied social forces, without questioning the overall system, if one leaves aside the Communist movement. Here, India is till now in a

---

15. Statement in 1999 during a Seminar on Labour issues and research in Delhi. Compare also the article by Thorat, Sukhadeo K. (1999). "Poverty, Caste and Child Labour in India: The Plight of Dalit and Adivasi Children", in Voll *op. cit.* pp.154-175

16. Voll, Klaus (1987). "Child Labour in the 18th and 19th Centuries: The German experience", in Manju Gupta and Klaus Voll (eds.), *Young Hands at Work: Child Labour in India*. Delhi/ Lucknow: Atma Ram & Sons. pp.69-90

disadvantage, since the extreme cleavages between the so-called "organised" and "un-organised" sectors, the pre-dominantly party-affiliated role of various Trade Unions, which have been for decades in their top ranks, completely in the grip of professional, external and mostly Brahminical and other upper-caste leaders, are far more a barrier than an avenue for the social and economic emancipation of *Dalits* and other socially disadvantaged sections.

Perhaps the intensifying "belated industrial revolution", so Oliver Müller, South Asia correspondent of the prestigious German economic daily *Handelsblatt,* could accelerate the decades old "silent revolution" (M.N. Srinivas), combined with an expansion of the "second democratic upsurge" (Yogendra Yadaw) in an era of increased foreign direct investments in India. It has to be seen, if continuous economic growth rates will have an impact on the living conditions of *Dalits* and other disadvantaged social sections. The growing requirements for qualified factory workers and craftsmen could open up wider venues for different sections of society, with the projection of inherent age-old dignity and skills, like in the past in the transition from guilds to specialised workers training in Europe.

Europeans between Lack of Interest and Concerns

The vast majority of Europeans currently living in India show overall no real concern for those, who are at the receiving end of the "in-built structural force" in India's society and its political power-system, although there are also a few laudable exceptions, which hopefully practice what they advocate and do not remain only declamatory. At the official level, Europeans overwhelmingly prefer to deal with the political, economic, social and cultural protagonists of the predominantly urban and upper-caste elite. They are, (un-) knowingly (?) or willingly, undoubtedly discriminatory "casteists"—let us exclude for the purpose of the argument the lack of sufficient interactions with Muslims and other religious minorities—and do not provide any or definitely insufficient job opportunities within their organisations and offices in India, to people outside the spectrum of the "twice-born", e.g. the upper-castes. They are, as it is for instance so evident within the UN-organisations, firmly in the hands of networks of these sections of the privileged elite, which indirectly also reflects the bias of the educational system, particularly in higher education. Therefore, it could be already a tremendous achievement, if Europeans would, in the areas where they still command influence, positively discriminate also in favour of NGO's led by Dalits themselves, besides others led by persons not belonging to the privileged upper-castes, and to award in particular also individual scholarships to such sections of society.

Yet, well-meaning European and Western friends of India[17] do express their concerns about the extreme inequalities and various discriminations within the multiple layers of Indian society and their many sub-societies and strata. Born out of Europe's historical experiences, the statement, "If You don't mobilize Your backwards, You Yourself will become internationally backward,"[18] appeals also to the collective self-interest of the Indian elite and the middle classes in particular, in order to realize the full use of the existing manpower potential in India on its way to a major global role and to reduce unnecessary social costs. After all, India will possess in a relatively short historical time frame a bigger work-force than the faster ageing and less growing People's Republic of China, besides becoming the state with the biggest population world-wide.

One can observe even today, in the era of globalisation, a dysfunctional waste of energies and time on the part of the urban upper- and middle classes, which are more or less identical with upper castes, to dilute adequate discussion about social reforms and the improvement of the situation of the Dalits. Instead, India requires at its current historical stage a new "social formula" (Gaetano Mosca) or "social contract", in order to mobilise its full potential with the participation of the entire social strata. Here, political foundations and established cultural organisations could exercise an influence with true inter-cultural dialogues between India and various European countries.

---

17. "True" friends of India are certainly those, who do not emphasise in a one-sided manner the projection of growth-rates without deeper thoughts to the social and ecological consequences.
18. This statement has been frequently used by me (Hans-Georg Wieck) in conversations with leading Indian politicians during my years as Ambassador to India between 1990 till 1993.

Political Assumptions and Wider Perspectives

After independence, the Congress Party, which ruled India uninterruptedly till 1977, co-opted the then existing Dalit leadership and received—as a part of its various caste-alliances—over a long period a tremendous percentage of *Dalit* votes. The efforts of Dr. Ambedkar, to create through the Republican Party of India (RPI) also an own political identity for Dalits failed over the years, caused by a lack of a Pan-Indian presence and by numerous splits.

In 1984, after the formation of the Bahujan Samaj Party (BSP), Atal Bihari Vajpayee, earlier India's Foreign—and later its Prime Minister, had been quoted in the political journal *India Today* with the following statement: "The formation of the Bahujan Samaj Party will transform fundamentally the political landscape of Northern India." This political foresight proved to be valid in particular for Uttar Pradesh, the most populous state of the Indian Union with about 160 million inhabitants, where BSP leader Mayawati led three times short-lived coalition governments and where the BSP is considered a major well-entrenched political force, since its 2007 overwhelming electoral success, more than ever before. Yet till now, the BSP could make only very limited inroads in states like Madhya Pradesh,[19] Uttarakhand and Punjab, not to speak of other parts of India.[20] As a consequence, the BSP, originally very clear in its rejection of the political and social influence of the upper-castes and their (*Manuvadi*) parties,[21] tries increasingly to appeal, besides its traditional support-basis of Dalits, *Chamars* in particular, and amongst sections of the Muslim electorate, to parts of the upper-castes and particularly to the relatively numerous Brahmins in Uttar Pradesh. Perhaps, nascent elements of a Dalit Social Democracy can be discerned, although neither the late Kanshi Ram nor his disciple Mayawati, a former school-teacher but now a powerful politician in her own right, have been ideologically very differentiated, and disregarded respective attempts at ideological and intellectual inputs with the aim of further ideological sophistication.

---

19. Pai, Sudhai (2005). "Political Mobilisation: A Comparative Study of Uttar Pradeh and Madhya Pradesh", in Debroy and Babu *op. cit.* p.213.

20. Interestingly, the BSP gained for the first time about 10 per cent in the elections to the Municipal Corporation in New Delhi in April 2007.

21. Ram, Kanshi (1982). *The Chamcha Age: The Era of Stooges.* New Delhi

Many mainstream parties and particularly the Communist Party of India/Marxist (CPI/M) are uncomfortable with the existence of the BSP and want to submerge the Dalit-question into the wider notion of "class". The CPI/M, the "last bastion of political Brahminism"[22], and also not the Communist Party of India (CPI) have really raised the Dalit issue adequately. When the late Indrajit Gupta, then General Secretary of the CPI, raised this question in the 1990's and demanded representation of Dalits etc., in leading positions of his party, there was a storm of protests. Interestingly, the CPI indicated support after the forthcoming Uttar Pradesh elections for a potentially led BSP-government.

The largest empirical research in the 1990's clearly demonstrated, that Dalits used their voting rights as a deliberate weapon and a kind of last resort within the Indian power system. Particularly in Uttar Pradesh, Dalit voters are alienated from the BJP and Congress, pan-Indian parties, yet with a limited country-wide reach. It will be interesting to observe, if this trend will continue in the 2007 election in this state or if the looming danger of a renewed religiously inspired and communal fundamentalism, trying to project the enemy within and targeting Indian citizens of Muslim religious belief, will raise its ugly head again, as it happened 1992 in Ayodhya and 2002 in Gujarat, which could also lead to religiously inspired fascist tendencies to avoid urgent and overdue economic and social reforms. Therefore, "the integration of Dalits into Indian Society—a key question for the Future of Indian Democracy"[23] is a most relevant issue for the rise of India as a stable and important global player in the International System of the 21st century, similar to the often painful processes of integration of disadvantaged sections into various societies in Europe in the 19th and 20th centuries. The situation of Dalits constitutes a part of India's backyard of extreme under-development, which in the medium- and long-term is not really presentable to the outside world, given its aspirations to be a future world-power and its recognisably growing cultural influence. Given its vast historical experience in its long-

22. A notion coined by me, Klaus Voll

23. This is the English translation of an article in the German language byWieck, Hans-Georg (2005). *"Die Integration der Dalits in die indische Gesellschaft—Eine Schlüsselfrage für die Zukunft der indischen Demokratie"*, in Herausgegeben von Günter Schucher und Christian Wagner, *Indien 2005: Politik-Wirtschaft-Gesellschaft*. Hamburg: Institut für Asienkunde. Seite 301-14

drawn processes of industrialisation, Europe's central heritage and message emanating from the 18th, 19th and 20th centuries are that social change in favour of disadvantaged sections of society are a central precondition for powerful and cohesive states in the wider context of the International System, which would also be in the interest of increased relations between the European Union and India, in the years and decades to come.